FILM IN THE AURA OF ART

1

2

3

4

5

6

7

8

FILM IN THE
AURA OF ART

DUDLEY ANDREW

PRINCETON UNIVERSITY PRESS

Publication of this book has been aided by a grant from
The Andrew W. Mellon Foundation
This book has been composed in Linotron Sabon

Clothbound editions of Princeton University Press books
are printed on acid-free paper, and binding materials
are chosen for strength and durability
Printed in the United States of America by
Princeton University Press
Princeton, New Jersey

"The theater," says Baudelaire, "is a chandelier."
If one were called upon to offer in comparison
a symbol other than this artificial crystal object,
brilliant, intricate, and circular, which refracts
the light which plays around its center and holds
us prisoners of its aureole, we might say of the
cinema that it is the little light of the usher,
moving like an uncertain comet across the night
of our waking dream, the diffuse space with
neither shape nor frontiers which surrounds the
screen.

Andre Bazin, "Theater and Cinema II"

That which withers in the age of mechanical reproduction is the aura of the work of art. . . .
This phenomenon is most palpable in the great
historical films. It extends to ever new positions.
In 1927 Abel Gance exclaimed enthusiastically:
"Shakespeare, Rembrandt, Beethoven will make
films . . . all legends, all mythologies and all
myths, all founders of religion, and the very re-
ligions . . . await their exposed resurrection, and
the heroes crowd each other at the gate." Presumably without intending it, he issued an invitation to a far-reaching liquidation.

Walter Benjamin,
"The Work of Art in the
Age of Mechanical Reproduction"

CONTENTS

ACKNOWLEDGMENTS

M INE is a book conceived as a conversation between film and viewer, viewer and reader, reader and text. While I can't hope to enumerate its complete dramatis personae, this conversation would certainly have sputtered without the textual presence of Paul Ricoeur and the educated interest of Stanley Cavell and my colleagues Steven Ungar, Pamela Falkenberg, and Gerald Bruns.

I am most grateful to Joanna Hitchcock, who recognized the unity and ambition of this project and who, along with Marilyn Campbell, saw it through to its publication. Chris Brenneman, Steven Dykes, Nancy Burkholder, and Stephanie Andrew helped bring the manuscript into its final form.

To Stephanie I am, as always, more than grateful. Her presence reminds me that this work has been more than work and that its fruits belong to those with whom, around whom—in whose aura—I have watched these films and been driven to discuss them. To our friends, then, I dedicate this book; or really to the personal life of culture the name of which is friendship and to the chief emanations of its aura in my life: to Judy, Robin, Dennis, Charlie, Steve, and Franklin, and to all the other figures traced on the mural of my memory.

PREFACE

T H E essays in this book grew out of my own distrust of pure film theory. More than five years ago I determined to study as deeply as possible many of the films that had led me to want to know about cinema in the first place. If the years I had spent studying theory couldn't aid my understanding of the power and mechanisms of those films, then something must be amiss. In fact I quickly found myself in the midst of a counterflow that led me back from the films to theory, until I reached the conclusion that film theory, at least those aspects of it that have always fascinated me, progresses only to the extent that it pursues problems uncovered in the close study of fertile films. This, by the way, is precisely the conclusion I draw chapter after chapter in my recent *Concepts in Film Theory*, a purely theoretical undertaking.

The impurity of this book is precisely what interests me, as elaborate readings of important films demand the confrontation of significant problems in theory. The problems (involving questions of representation, the place of the spectator, narrative structure, the ontology of images and sounds, and the sociology of art) beg exploration, not systematically, but only as they arise in the terms put forth by the films. This interplay between theory and criticism, if not natural, has at least the form of a dialogue in which the films have the first word and, frequently, the last.

What sorts of films command the kind of respect I am according them? As the epigraphs so tantalizingly hint, cinema entered the world of serious art only after having altered that world forever. Can cinema command our attention and imagination today in the way that, say, classical theater did for an earlier age? Bazin and Benjamin, for very different reasons, sense a complete break in the function of art brought about by the motion pictures; the aura and the aureole have vanished. Yet far from distressing these men, the cinema excited them. Art is renewed in the secular light of the cinema; might secular man be renewed by this new art? Like Bazin and Benjamin, all the films studied in this volume are obsessed by the tradition of art behind them and by a mass audience before them.

But to group these films under the rubric "art cinema," as I provisionally do, is a subterfuge, for if they form a genre, its only rule is that each member of that genre develop its own rules. This is why they interest me. Teasing out those rules and displaying their consequences for cinema as a whole is essentially the project of this book. I'd like to think that this is a most natural project, an obvious posture for any student or enthusiast of the movies to take. If the academic discipline of film studies consists of films, methods of reading them, theories about films, and the historical relations that bind all these, then mine seek to be comprehensive essays. Whatever intrigues me in the discipline ought to come up as I set out to see how far and in what directions these films carry me, these films I have chosen or (as I persist in claiming) these films that have chosen me.

In this age of doubt and self-doubt, no one is permitted to bask in the belief that theirs is a natural project or that the films they study have reached out to make an unavoidable claim on them. Thus the general reflections on art and interpretation that serve to introduce and conclude this volume were forced by the intellectual climate in which we all live. There I struggle to justify my choice of films and methods. If, as is now commonly held, all texts are equal and all readings proceed less from logic and intention than from "reading formations" proper to their cultural moment, then this and all similar studies are at once arbitrary and determined. In any case they are evaluatively neutral.

The debilitating consequences of this view require countering. My effort to argue for a choice of films and for a kind of discourse about them must set itself against the powerful claims made by followers of Foucault and Derrida. I find that ultimately film study does not in any useful sense belong to cultural philosophy, and that its very struggle to exist against one or another skeptical imperialism is enough to justify it. Films, readings of them, and theories about both are historical *events in* culture, not replaceable *functions of* culture. Or so I believe. The essays that follow demonstrate, more or less adequately and eloquently, that belief. Culture exists only as values read by its subjects. Like all interpretation, my essays are a conversation within culture, not an argument about culture. I will not deny that their enthusiasm betrays my belief in the efficacy of choice and the value of history, although such enthusiasm comes not at all from some abstract notion of historical value, about which I, like most of us, have grave doubts. No, it is the particular encounters I have had with films, people, and discourse, that have driven me to write and, in writing, to promote, while trying to alter, a culture that in some measure we all share.

I HOPE the pictures grouped in the center of the volume will thicken the readings of the films. With the cooperation of the Museum of Modern Art and the British Film Institute I have selected a few stills from every film discussed and in some cases a great many. Glance over these stills before looking through any chapter, just to involve memory and visual imagination. They have been arranged more by theme and complementarity than by strict attention to the chronology of the plots. And most often these are the themes and visual relationships I emphasize in the text. As often as appropriate, then, I signal the relevance of the stills by inserting in the text a bracketed number corresponding to the still from the page or pages of pictures devoted to that chapter.

The frontispiece needs special mention since, aside from serving to illustrate the chapter on *Henry V*, it proposes to set the tone for the book as a whole. Stills from Olivier's film line up on the left column alongside some of the artworks that film emulates. Still 4 might serve as an allegory or argument for my whole enterprise since it features a purely cinematic concoction designed to pay homage to art, not to cinema. Olivier here portrays Jean, Duc de Berri, a character not mentioned at all by Shakespeare, but the man responsible for the illuminated manuscripts which are the source for much of the film's set design. In signaling us with his finger to look into the book he cradles in his arm, this character invites cinema to lose itself in exquisite images and words. I point in the same way to the films I treat and, more modestly, to the words and pictures you now hold in your hands.

Iowa City
September 1983

FILM IN THE
AURA OF ART

CHAPTER ONE

Introduction: The Art Cinema and the Work of Interpretation

> The single text is valid for all the texts of
> literature, not in that it represents them
> (abstracts and equalizes them), but in that
> literature itself is never anything but a single
> text: the one text is not an (inductive) access to
> a Model, but entrance into a network with a
> thousand entrances; to take this entrance is to
> aim, ultimately, not at a legal structure of
> norms and departures, a narrative or poetic
> Law, but at a perspective (of fragments, of
> voices from other texts, other codes), whose
> vanishing point is nonetheless ceaselessly pushed
> back, mysteriously opened; each (single) text is
> the very theory (and not the mere example) of
> this vanishing, of this difference which
> indefinitely returns, insubmissive.
> —Roland Barthes, *S/Z*

JUST how do films make meaning? How does such meaning come to interest us? These may seem like questions
(primary questions) of film theory, but they arise in any serious
treatment of film. For this very reason the work of theorists
and critics of cinema has increasingly overlapped in our era.
Most outstanding has been the attempt to discover basic laws
of film's grammar, including its psychoanalytical attraction
and social function, through the analysis of what we have
come to term "classic" films. In such analyses the films are
treated wholly for their exemplary force. It is the system that
is at stake, be it a semiotic, psychoanalytic, or ideological

system, and the films are scrutinized for the light they shed on aspects of these systems.

The essays in this collection announce a different relation of theory and criticism by according to films a more authoritative status. Let us take seriously Barthes' tantalizing assertion that the text can be not an example but the theory itself. Then we must respond to the film, teasing out its method and appeal as it displays that method and makes that appeal. While key issues in theory are addressed in these essays (issues such as representation, structure, adaptation, figure, and, most insistently, spectator position) the logic of theory follows the movement of the films. This is not only possible, it is demanded by the films themselves, which call for rich and varied readings. In this way, instead of being absorbed back into the system, these films continue to "open up" before us as we fly toward their vanishing point. We try to grasp them but find them perpetually "insubmissive."

Each of the films dealt with in this book dares to approach us with its difference from the system of standard films, dares to promise to affect us in unique and privileged ways, hoping to attain thereby a certain importance if not immortality.

What shall we say of such claims and such films? We must first confront the sociology of art to ascertain the status and function of these films before responding to them in the way that they press us to do. To what extent does that "difference" which Barthes ascribes to literary texts apply to films made in a vigorously controlled economic market? If feature films operate under a strict system, a purely deductive theory or grammar should adequately account for them as products. This would seem to be the case in the pop music field, and even (or especially) with TV shows. Who would think of according an episode of a TV series the kind of respect Barthes gives to Balzac? Generally we treat these media generically, saying that we want to "watch TV" or "put on a record." The art film, on the contrary, wants to make us choose to enter the theater just as we decide to go to a concert featuring Beethoven's sonata opus 111. If for years spectators around the world simply went out to the movies, the art film, even in these years, sought to differentiate itself from their common experience.

Of course, after the advent of TV the film industry as a whole began to use this rhetoric of "the unique experience," hoping to lure audiences to fewer but bigger films. A familiar rule of adjustment came into play when many films began to advertise themselves on the basis of their uniqueness. We can read ads from the fifties up to our own day luring us to see one "absolutely different kind of film" after another. The genre of the unique film, then, is not so very different from standard genres which have always invited us to experience something new within the familiar. Obviously this is the crux of the economy of cinema, promising something at once the same and different.

Even if all feature films participate in this economy of sameness and difference, we must approach the genre of the art film with special care, for these films appeal to a wholly new audience or a new sensibility in the standard audience. Certainly this appeal stems, like all generic appeals, from a desire to win over a large audience. These so-called "distinctive" works have most often banded together under a classy rubric (such as "film d'art" or "impressionism") just to distinguish themselves in a battle against the innumerable products of Hollywood. Several European industries even accorded special economic status to their export films. In France and England the words "Cinema of Quality" connoted art, elegance, and a certain difference vis-à-vis the large numbers of genre films produced by those countries and the much larger number of such films made in Hollywood. American audiences grew to expect distinct characteristics from such foreign imports, which invariably played at "art houses," at least after World War II.

Yet, despite the fact that these films played in a regulated way to a distinct audience much as do sci-fi films or children's fare, the art cinema promises something no other group of films can: to question, change, or disregard standard filmmaking in seeking to convey or discover the utterly new or the formerly hidden. It is under this promise that these films claim a right to perpetual interest and existence. While today we may cast a suspicious eye on the romantic rhetoric associated with great artworks, there can be little doubt that this ambitious impulse helped produce many of the films that challenge us today because they challenged the system in which they were produced.

The essays in this volume take up the challenge of those films that insist on being different. Purportedly outside the system, they must teach us how to deal with them. This they do in the midst of our viewing them, or, more often, as we feel called to re-view them. The effort they demand of spectators to learn a new system, one suitable for a single film, places the film outside standard cinema where it may be either ignored or given special, even lasting, attention.

THE FILMS

Many films have claimed this special status, even in the classic era (1920-1960) and even in the conservative, marketable mode of the feature fiction film. As the medium changed and the sociology of art evolved, different rubrics promoted different films as exceptional. The essays in this book sample all decades of the classic era and films deriving from various sources. Some are standard big-money studio projects (*Sunrise, The Magnificent Ambersons, Henry V*) while others are intimate productions crafted by renegades under unique circumstances (*L'Atalante, Diary of a Country Priest, Chimes at Midnight*). But in all cases the films continue to interest us for having modified our notion of the cinema or, through the cinema, our representation of life.

Until 1940 the most ambitious films felt the need to start from an original script. This was the era in which the "specificity" of cinema seemed to be at stake in every important film. The first four essays in this book concern films struggling to find a proper balance between story and image. The scripts for *Broken Blossoms, Sunrise,* and *L'Atalante* outline simple plots while making room for significant plastic development. Griffith, we shall see, equated complex plotting with the crasser function of the medium and reserved special affection for the delicate photography and imagistic sophistication of *Broken Blossoms,* his one art film. *Sunrise,* deriving from a marriage of expressionism and Hollywood, sought a nearly operatic relation to its audience, complete with an allegorical plot line. *L'Atalante* likewise found a new balance of image to story, but it did so within the aesthetic of the avant-garde tradition rather than the classic aesthetic of *Sunrise* or the melodramatic one of *Broken Blossoms.* All three films implicitly set themselves against the heavily plotted and dialogued fare of Hollywood. But even within the Hollywood system it was possible for a film to seek to stand apart. *Meet John Doe* is a perfect example here, designed as it was to attack the system through the system.

Of all the films treated in this book, Capra's comes closest to the standard product, differing, if at all, in the implications of its "message." For as World War II started, Capra, along with most of the movie-making world, was convinced that the medium had indeed developed its specific powers, so much so that a serious film could now be literally written for production. But 1940 found other directors arguing the opposite. This is the watershed moment, according to André Bazin, in which the deep-focus styles of Renoir and Welles tipped film language away from its obsessive self-concern and toward the subjects it was its mission to render.[1]

One such subject was the serious book or play. Formerly mere timber for the studio sawmills whose scriptwriters rebuilt them into properly cinematic structures, certain literary works were now approached with reverence for their stylistic integrity and appeal. This necessarily forced ambitious filmmakers to seek new cinematic solutions in order to bring them intact

[1] André Bazin, "In Defense of Mixed Cinema," *What is Cinema?* trans. Hugh Gray (Berkeley and Los Angeles: University of California Press, 1968).

to the screen. It is not happenstance, then, that the second four essays in this book treat adaptations, for by 1940 this issue drew the same sort of broad and intelligent concern that the issue of "specificity" had held for the preceding era.

Bazin's own country was an important site in the development of a new ethic of adaptation and a battleground over the aesthetics this ethic involved. Jean Delannoy's clever but conventional rendering of the Gide *Symphonie pastorale* came into sharp conflict with Robert Bresson's highly personal *Diary of a Country Priest*, a film so rigorous that Bresson once announced that he expected no more than 10,000 spectators to really appreciate it. Bresson had to fight Delannoy's scriptwriters for the opportunity to direct *Diary*. Soon afterwards he lost a battle with Delannoy himself over the rights to another French classic, *La Princesse de Cleves*. As Bazin had predicted, the struggle over adaptation had the widest possible consequences, for it involved conceptions of the style and function of cinema as a whole. This particular skirmish played an important role in the overall campaign waged by the New Wave critics against "le cinema du papa."[2]

In the English-speaking world, adaptation has most frequently been discussed in relation to Shakespeare, and here Olivier's *Henry V* still stands out as the most original and well-known of such films. Coming at the close of World War II, Olivier challenged a huge audience (the film played for a full year in continuous run at New York's Paris Theater) with a most disjunctive visual style. A fantastically successful studio product, this film contradicts the common assumption that films of great appeal must promote an illusionistic mode of representation.

Olivier's approach to adaptation, to Shakespeare, and to cinema was opposed after the war by an actor of equal fame,

---

[2] Of course the most important essay in this campaign, Truffaut's "A Certain Tendency in French Cinema," directly addresses the crisis of adaptation and calls on Bresson's film for support. This essay appears in Bill Nichols, ed., *Movies and Methods* (Berkeley and Los Angeles: University of California Press, 1976).

Orson Welles. In *Macbeth* and *Othello* he found himself fully at odds with Olivier's practice. First of all, Welles operated with budgets only a fraction of those of his English counterpart; but more important, his sense of cinema's obligation to the bard couldn't have been more different. His 1966 masterpiece, *Chimes at Midnight*, brings out this opposition clearly, for it dares in the first place to tamper with the sacred text and then to set that text inside a space so deep that it muffles the verse. *Henry V* had gloried in its various levels of artifice and had excited an audience ready to adjust to its overt theatricality because this was sanctioned by the holy name of Shakespeare. Twenty years later Welles' film failed utterly at the box office due perhaps to his irreverently realistic treatment of this same Shakespeare, whose poetry is often lost in the great tunnel Welles makes of the screen.

The nearly metaphysical authorial tone Welles achieves in *Chimes at Midnight* is not limited to his Shakespeare films, nor to his adaptations of exotic and prized literary animals (Kafka's *The Trial*, Isak Dinesen's *Immortal Story*, the half-completed *Don Quixote*). Welles' deep seriousness, in fact, is never more disturbing than in his second film, *The Magnificent Ambersons*. In his extraordinary career this seemingly ordinary subject remains the privileged film, not because it forestalls the extraneous issue of Welles' screen personality, but because, far more than even *Meet John Doe*, it is on its face a standard Hollywood production. Deriving from a Pulitzer-Prize-winning novel, and set in mid-America of the early 1900s, this film promises nothing exceptional. Yet, next to *Meet John Doe* it is a revolution, for while his subject may have been more conventional than Capra's, Welles' method lay outside the system, so much so that he was soon forced physically out of Hollywood to roam Europe looking for patrons eager to support cinema in the way painting and music have always been supported on that continent.

Welles must serve as America's most notable specimen of the ambitious filmmaker, bucking the system to the limit, associating himself with literary masterworks, creating a per-

sonal and identifiable style of sound and image. In the ear-
nestness of his demeanor he resembles many other international artists, for example, Bergman, Antonioni, and Dreyer.
This book of essays closes with a study of Kenji Mizoguchi,
who on first blush would appear to belong to this group of
isolated film artists. But Mizoguchi, perhaps alone in the history of world cinema, not only earned a reputation for in-
novation, rigor, and high art, but he did so while sitting dead
center in one of the world's greatest film systems. Mizoguchi
was undoubtedly the strongest single personal force in that
system for over thirty years, yet he challenged and upset the
Japanese film style decade after decade. His recalcitrant nature
and the even more recalcitrant nature of his great films provide us with a final meditation on the sociology of art implicit
in the selections of this book. For Mizoguchi displays not only
a different style and subject matter than we in the West have
ever encountered, he demands perhaps a new conception of
the very activity of filmmaking and film viewing, a conception
potentially at odds with what we have come to know in the
West, whether in the standard cinema of genres or in what
we have tried to describe here as the ambitious cinema of art.

THE READINGS

Despite the range of ambitious films sampled in this book,
my purpose has not been historical or sociological. Rather, I
have sought to exercise an unusually tenacious brand of interpretation on films that promise to reward such labor. Edification should be the result, the kind of edification each film
in its singularity can offer, and that other kind of edification
brought about by the generalizing power of film theory; for
each essay, while sticking close to the movements and hints
of the film under scrutiny, strives to bring to light the conditions, and method, by which meaning and significance come
to us in our experience of the movies.
    The double reward, from the films and from the generali-
zations made possible by the films, springs, I have argued,

from the "difference" these works maintain from standard cinema. Surely all films require interpretation, especially if, along with most modern writers on the subject, we agree that culture is nothing other than a vast forum of interpretations. But the kind of interpretation required by the genre film is utterly distinct from that demanded by the ambitious film. The genre film reads itself, passing smoothly through the viewer into the canon of the acceptable. Discourse about such films is superfluous at the primary level, for everything, even the enigma of the plot, ultimately makes sense. It is only at a higher level of abstraction that we can be interested. That level, film theory, will try to reproduce the rules of the system by which this film, and all others of its kind, make up for us an unquestioned representation of life.

The films treated in this book do not read themselves and do not, at least initially, seem to answer to the rules theory has constructed for standard cinema. Interpretation in these cases plays a more obvious role, for it must necessarily try to reconcile the new to the known, the deviation to the system.

We tend to think of standard cinema as offering entertainment and cohesion as it pretends to expand our experience. We watch another detective film to enjoy the sense of order brought about by the solution to the crime, but also to test our curiosity against the new crimes, new motivations, new geographies that form the subjects of such films. Even horror films perform this function as they allow us to try to integrate the greatest of unknowns and our worst fears into the order of our lives.

Such new experience comes for the most part along very familiar channels, the channels of genre and of the film system in general, and this familiarity is what makes integration so easy and comforting. While some alteration or development in the system keeps each film from being exactly like its predecessors, all novelty is carefully regulated so as not to disturb our sense of the intelligibility and authority operating in the films.

The art film, however, is more insistently different, disrupting integral vision and cohesiveness. Most often the impetus for us to permit such disruption comes only from our respect for the authentic vision of the creator, as when we believe Bresson to have a fully *other* sense of values, one that we feel drawn to try to adopt, if only as an experiment.

Now, a romantic view of serious art holds that the greatest works lead us out of our habitual ways of seeing things and allow us to touch a more profound reality via a more complicated and interesting representation. Merle Brown has argued that interpretation is systematic within authentic artworks; that is, that every poem of consequence listens to itself, adjusts itself to the possible meanings opening up before it, so that the finished poem is a record of an internal hermeneutic process.[3] Even if we are not prepared to go this far, we have been taught, certainly since Heidegger, that value and meaning in art come from the role played by the reader who adjusts a web of interpretations to accommodate the body of the poem. The physicality of the work regulates and directs (at the same time that it invites) the movement toward meaning, at least in artworks of the highest ambition.

But how radically new are such films and the insights they promise? The regulation of new information, including both its incorporation into a dominant system and the adjustment of the system to significantly new information, is a process that describes the longevity of our way of life. Capitalism, liberal democracy, and the ideology they promote thrive on change and adjustment. From this perspective the so-called deviant art films are essential to the renovation of the system, for its suppleness in dominating history and change. So that from the modern perspective, no film, particularly no fiction film of feature length, can be thought of or treated apart from the economic and aesthetic system of film in general.[4]

---

[3] Merle Browne, "Poetic Listening," *New Literary History* 10 (Autumn 1978), 125-40.

[4] Pamela Falkenberg has been responsible for my views of the subject via personal conversation and a series of papers written at The University of Iowa.

But whether we approach art films reverentially or cynically, as promising salvation through a new vision or in delivering the "same old newness" to an inexorable system, one thing is clear: these works demand a type of critical activity not required of more standard cinema. Despite the historical circumstances out of which each arose, despite the tainted and partial sense of the word "art" by which each has sought to justify itself and its audience, the films this volume treats call for repeated viewing and privileged, serious discussion. To reabsorb them completely into the system under the blanket rubric "ideology" is to refuse that call and thereby to assert once more the power of the theorist over the films themselves.

It is precisely here, situated between the conflicting demands of ambitious theory on the one hand and of ambitious films on the other, that film criticism, or interpretation, must come to the aid of both. For interpretation seeks always to adjust the knower to the known, altering both in the process. Whether it be relating a new film to our standard conception of film or to the rules that we thought governed all films, interpretation is a process that asserts the value of both knowledge and experience, giving precedence to neither. Its end is adequation, not objective truth.

But let us not minimize the value of adequation. Even the most trenchantly doctrinaire of modern theorists would agree that these films marshalled a new audience (or a new sensibility of the standard audience), promising pleasure through the disruption and deformation of the system. In bringing about new codes to permit their own reading these films did not so much abolish the system (or bypass it) as establish themselves in relation to it. In other words, these films would be unreadable without the system whose sameness they hope to escape. Interpretation reconciles this tension between the system and the event of a new film.

In this way film criticism must no longer be seen as a parasitic enterprise engaged in by the effete to prolong their pleasure or confirm their superiority. Criticism, as the institutionalized form of interpretation, is central to the construction of meaning itself as it is formed in the give and take between tradition and the encounter of the new.[5]

Film theory had thought to account deductively for the process of understanding a film, at best employing examples from standard films to confirm its hypotheses. And yet the film system is only the sedimentation of interpretations built up habitually over the years. There is no objective truth about signification in films, only a tradition of reading them in such and such a way, a tradition most films rely upon and exploit without hesitation. The demise of a rigid film semiotics in the face of poetics and rhetoric confirms the centrality of interpretation even at the most basic level of signification. Originally semioticians felt they could establish a semblance of a film grammar so that clear denotations could be ascribed to various signifiers. But the knotty issue of connotation continually encroached on this grammar until it became clear that all signification in cinema originates through the interpretation of connotation and of figures. If certain conventions attain the stability of denotation (a fade-out indicating a change of time or location) it is only thanks to its repeated figural use in the early history of film.

The mechanism of signification in the cinema, then, is most readily available not to pure reflection or logical schemes, but to the reading of figures in those films history has delivered to us. This is an especially productive strategy when applied to the art film because of its announced program of going against the grain of standard cinematic practice. In interpreting difficult films we construct their meaning while simultaneously exposing the conventional cinematic language that they seek to transcend or employ to new ends.

Central to the enterprise of film theory, interpretation is more crucial to the strong films it brings to light, for the life of art depends both on the viewer and on the artifact viewed, on the system and on the event put into play by the new work.

[5] I argue this position at length throughout *Concepts in Film Theory*, particularly in the final chapter (New York: Oxford University Press, 1984).

No longer can we pretend to approve, by fiat, a canon of seminal films whose meaning is patently valuable to us or to our culture. It is interpretation, even what Ricoeur calls the "conflict of interpretations,"[6] that, through give and take between the work and the viewer, constitutes both the tradition and the promise of meaning, and that therefore is the surest index of value. Inasmuch as a work generates discourse, it is involved in the meaning of culture and is, by definition, valuable. The community decides which works merit discussion, and these may change over time. But the choice is not arbitrary, as certain modernist thinkers would have it. Rather the culture, in its particular historical moment, responds to the insistence and urgency it senses within certain films, those that, for whatever reason, seem to call to the culture. What is this urgency, this promise of meaning, and why do certain films insist so strongly on our response? This is exactly what is to be discovered in interpretation. Dependent at once on the films and on theory, the essays which follow are on the road to such discovery.

[6] Paul Ricoeur, *The Conflict of Interpretations* (Evanston: Northwestern University Press, 1975).

CHAPTER TWO

Broken Blossoms: The Vulnerable Text and the Marketing of Masochism

UNQUESTIONABLY while the institution of cinema has always harbored "artists" of various sorts and a set of practices known as "the art of the film," nevertheless only a select number of its products have been labeled "art films." As early as the turn of the century the business community was quick to capitalize on the advertising potential in the word "art" and applied it to distinguish those products that were fictional or dramatic from those that appealed to the more sensational or curious side of its potential audience. For example, the French "Film d'Art" Company hoped by its very name to lure a high-class audience to its re-creations of dramatic masterpieces performed by the renowned tragedians of the day.

But here, as was the case during the cinema's first twenty-five years of existence, art was thought of not as something cinematic, but as something one put into a film: famous actors, a serious drama. D. W. Griffith's *Intolerance* of 1916 changed this situation only superficially. For while he first garnered attention for the composition of the film, for the artistry of its construction, the true art of *Intolerance* was seen as a set of rhetorical devices "added to" a serious moral drama to intensify and uplift its message and to increase respect for its speaker, Griffith himself.

This notion of art as "enhancement" of a worthy moral subject certainly served western civilization for many years, at least from Horace and Plutarch through the middle ages

This chapter was first published, in a slightly different form, in the *Quarterly Review of Film Studies* 6 (Winter 1981). Reprinted by permission of the editors.

and into the renaissance, but it is a notion distinctly set aside by the romantics and operable in cinema only to the extent that cinema does not participate in that set of institutions recognized today as "the fine arts."

Certainly the early cinema had its aestheticians, proclaiming the viability of film as a fine art. Hugo Munsterberg and Vachel Lindsay can quickly be cited. But it wasn't until the birth of the French impressionist movement in 1919 that a large subculture actively began treating cinema institutionally (not merely theoretically) as a fine art. Clubs, publications, manifestos, the sponsorship of short films, lectures, and exhibitions all fawned over certain privileged films and, more important, demanded new films based on contemporary standards of taste in painting, music, and the novel. The impressionists were an elite group fostering a conception of cinema that might appeal to an elite audience.

The year 1919 also saw the introduction of a more refined and self-conscious notion of cinematic art in America. It was predictably championed by Griffith and expressed by a single film, *Broken Blossoms*. Indeed it might be suggested that it was Griffith's megalomania, inflated by the fame he had achieved in 1916, that allowed this more acceptable notion of art to be admitted in America, where the sort of subculture of the French impressionists could never exist and where every alteration in the institution of cinema had to be ratified by the single dominating culture, Hollywood. It took someone of Griffith's stature as well as of his obtuseness to pass off a concept of cinema few studio businessmen could understand, let alone support.

The strictly economic pressures which doubtless set this film apart from Griffith's earlier efforts have been amply detailed by Arthur Lennig and Vance Kepley.[1] Far too short at eighty-

---

[1] Two excellent studies of the making of this film, both of which discuss the "artfilm" ambitions of Griffith, are Vance Kepley, "Griffith's *Broken Blossoms* and the Problem of Historical Specificity," *Quarterly Review of Film Studies* 3 (1978), 37-48; and Arthur Lennig, "*Broken Blossoms*, D. W. Griffith, and the Making of an Unconventional Masterpiece," *Film Journal* 2 (Fall-Winter 1978), 2-9.

five minutes to promote in the manner of the epics *Birth of a Nation* and *Intolerance, Broken Blossoms* also lacked the expansive heaving rhythms of those films. In truth, it was a minor undertaking from the standpoint of production. Shot in seventeen days, on only a few simple sets, its cost ($70,000) was a fraction of the earlier masterworks.

Yet Griffith was determined to invest his money and prestige to promote the film. Perhaps the snubs he received in arranging for its distribution set his resolve to ignore the normal promotional channels in Hollywood and supervise personally the distribution and exhibition of what had become for him a "pet child." This conflict with the establishment assuredly contributed to the self-righteous attitude Griffith adopted, and this attitude in turn gave rise to the concept of art as the criterion and category capable of locating the worth and appeal of this film. "Art" was thus a new weapon in an ongoing economic war, provided it could be sold to the public. Griffith was convinced that it could, for he presumed that the public would trust him and his sensibility, presumed that they would follow him on this new road, certain that with him they would reach a newer, better region of experience.

Griffith was clearly pleased with himself for having avoided the secure path to success, narrative and spectacle. He felt he was stretching the medium by demanding a new audience orientation for *Broken Blossoms*, an orientation capable of attending and responding to a new narrative ethos. For Griffith the novelty of this ethos lay in the delicate tone sustained through much of the film and culminating in the pathos of the suicide at the end. Here he helped draw up the audience contract that the genre of the "art film" has operated under ever since: the postponement or repression of the easy pleasures of spectacle and story in deference to those higher sensibilities that we bring into play when we respond to inspirational poetry, drama, painting, or music. The suicide, as a mark of unpleasure, guarantees the seriousness of the piece, while the placid and subtle narration, as a mark of sensitivity, insists on the uncompromising virtue of the author, his refusal to play on the usual and crass emotions and expectations of his audience.

Instead of dismissing Griffith's sanctimonious attitude, let us look with disinterest at his perceptions, to understand the development of the ethos in *Broken Blossoms* and its function in our experience. In Griffith's absolutely binary world, art was already associated with the quiet, the uplifting, the moral, the delicate, and (certainly for him) the feminine. He cushioned the opening of *Broken Blossoms* with a title pointing to its elevated status and precious subject: "It is a tale of tears." As Vance Kepley has documented,[2] Griffith invested significant amounts of time and money ornamenting the film so as to allow it to seduce its first audiences: he worked excessively on the film's music, on its tinting, on the surface lighting effects which were employed to bathe the screen in color at its first performances. Beyond this he arranged for the "Dance of Life and Death" routine, which served as a live-act prelude to fill out the otherwise brief program and which simultaneously invoked the high art tradition which that program hoped to situate itself within. The dance's universal philosophic subject was designed to appeal to "the several hundred patrons of the serious arts" who received invitations to these premieres.

Griffith felt he needed to control the very atmosphere in the theater to promote the values of art over entertainment. But in fact he probably needed nothing of the sort, for *Broken Blossoms*, while changing the terms of the conventional melodrama that Griffith had employed since his days at Biograph, did not change its essential structure. It was still a matter of posing antithetical values at the film's outset, arranging for audience identification on a given side, and then proceeding to a dramatic struggle in which the proper side as well as the audience would, after appropriate detours and delays, be rewarded. *Broken Blossoms* is built on the opposition between the Yellow Man and Battling Burrows, between the values of

[2] Kepley, "Griffith's *Broken Blossoms*," pp. 42-45.

China and those of London, between a contemplative passive
way of life and an aggressive violent way. Griffith could add,
for purposes of promotion, that these oppositions culminated
in a struggle within the audience between art and spectacle
so that the film became for him a melodramatic representation
of the fragility of art (and of the artist) in a culture dominated
by crass entertainment moguls. The violent plot itself, in other
words, not the delicate ornamentation dangling from it, was
enough to seduce an audience that had been raised on variants
of this plot. Griffith and his hesitant backers hadn't enough
confidence in the power of the violent structure of his films,
fearing that the unfamiliar locus of identification (oriental
values, art) and the bizarre plot permutation it demanded
(suicide) would turn this film away from the public. They
were wrong. Carrying its audience along, art triumphed in
this conflict, but a rather peculiar sort of art it was and an
even more peculiar sort of triumph.

The introductory sequence sets up this conflict in miniature
by pitting the serene Yellow Man, fresh from his temple retreat, against three feisty American sailors. The sailors know
no rule of life save rough and tumble fun, healthy unreflective
instincts. The Yellow Man, on the other hand, is shown to
be the product of a sophisticated culture and tradition. In the
establishing scenes before he is introduced, three marriageable
Chinese women, potential partners for the soldiers, routinely
consult an ancient fortuneteller in the streets. Against the brightly
lit contours of their youthful forms this man is presented in
a brooding sort of light and very shallow focus. His life, and
theirs, is measured by the book he points to, which Griffith
renders in extreme close-up. Similarly the beauty and brightness of the Yellow Man presents itself from the very first
within the sanctuary of an established order. The perfect symmetry of Griffith's découpage in the temple expresses clearly
the Yellow Man's strength and the source of that strength. In
the heart of this scene is a close-up of prayer beads followed
by an insert shot of a monk striking a gong and another of
several monks before a dominating Buddha. The Yellow Man's

teacher reads from a text as Griffith cuts back to his concluding long shots. Griffith thus doubles the mise-en-scène with an editing strategy that structures the Yellow Man permanently within this world of eternal values. His very motionlessness is testimony to the rightness of this world and of him, its worthy inheritor.

The many tableaux in this sequence are marked by subtly restful compositions and by the gauzy photographic style so crucial to the film later on. More important, they are marked *as* tableaux; that is, the dramatic power of the introduction is lodged in static representations rather than in any sequenced relationship of events.

In this first sequence the static is explicitly associated with the eternity of the Buddha and of the traditional texts which rule the lives of all citizens, especially that of the Yellow Man. This style of life, and the memory of its rule, will be carried over to London in the body of the film by means of acting, lighting, and camerawork. The slow posturing of the Asians contrasts strikingly in the introduction with the angular gesticulating of the sailors. Later this acting code will fall primarily on a nearly ludicrous opposition between the Yellow Man and Battling Burrows: the oriental's oblique liquid movements come to rest in gently curved poses which concentrate and contain the dramatic energy within the frame, while the burly boxer thrashes about abruptly and gracelessly, thrusting our attention out of the frame and to the object of his aggression.[3]

Battling Burrows is likewise an inverted measure for eastern lighting and compositional values. He is filmed in uniformly harsh light and nearly always in a shot long enough to place him in the context of other objects. The Yellow Man frequently is shot with the Sartov long-lens technique[4] or with curved masking, diffused lighting, or a black background. All

---

[3] My observations on acting in this film have been informed by Charles Affron, *Star Acting: Gish, Garbo, and Davis* (New York: Dutton, 1977), pp. 11-36.

[4] Lennig, "Broken Blossoms," p. 3.

of these techniques combine in certain key scenes, cutting him off from his physical context and etherealizing him and the kind of life he stands for.

The introductory sequence gives us time to grow accustomed to this new set of values so that we are ready to accept peace and stasis over our habitual love of violence and dynamism. Our reward for this choice is the pleasure specifically afforded by the contemplation of composed pictorial values. This pleasure the narrative ultimately delivers to us in the justly famous long-lens close-ups of Lillian Gish, shots that, we are told,[5] changed the nature of the close-up, the nature of the star, and perhaps the nature of cinematic pleasure itself.

The means by which Griffith displaced audience interest in story to audience involvement in static portraits of Lillian Gish comprises two movements. First she is pinched between the pressured glances of opposing forces; second, her own gaze in response buries itself in a series of self-reflections. Thus all visual and dramatic power is focused on her where it is held tight within the narcissism of her own perception. In a cruel world she dare not lift her eyes as a prelude to action or defense, instead latching on to fragile mirrors of herself until the accumulation of spectator and character libido invests the images of Gish with enough vibrating energy to illuminate the entire film with its fluorescence.

The specific mechanism of this displacement of narrative onto pictorial involvement begins with the immobilization of the heroine. From her first moment we see her caught between unacceptable alternatives. Sitting despondent on a rubble heap outside her Limehouse shack, she meditates on the choices the future leaves open to her: slaving for a flock of emaciated urchins or selling herself on the streets. Her current life is no less a tale of horrid alternatives: the brutality of Battling Burrows at home and the dangers of the vices in the oriental district when she wanders from home. Solace comes to her only in the few fragments of beauty she finds around her,

---

[5] *Ibid.*

fragments like the flowers and the tinfoil which cause her downcast eyes to lift in excitement.

One particular sequence embodies this structure consummately [1-8]. Wandering up to the Yellow Man's storefront window Lucy is oblivious to the pressure of gazes that effectively pin her to that window. From the inside the Yellow Man and from across the street Evil Eye transfix her, their glances competing with one another on the space of her body. Moments later when she crosses the street and stands next to Evil Eye while trading her foil for a flower, the Yellow Man follows her and balances the play of glances horizontally. A series of crosscuts makes the tension of this scene explicit and Lucy's position between these eyes unmistakable. Two inserts of Battling Burrows at a local pub remind us that there is no escape for Lucy. Caught between her father and the oriental district she is here caught within the oriental district.

Mercifully oblivious to this web of eyes that threaten her, Lucy for her part is absorbed in the delicate little objects reminiscent of her: the crumpled foil she unearthed from the floor, the store window where her own reflection now hovers beside a row of little girl dolls (one of which she will later crush to her breast), and, of course, the flowers, explicit metaphor of the film's title. If, in the conventions of cinema, glances are a prelude to the violence of narrative movement and action, if they invest characters and objects with differential value and vectorize the photographic space, then we must say of Lucy that she has internalized her desire by gazing only at herself, through the complicity of self-referring objects which ultimately condense into the hand mirror that absorbs her desire. The essential passivity of this response to the world cuts her off from positive action and makes her vulnerable to those at whose glare she casts down her eyes. It makes her, we must admit, vulnerable to our own intense view which seems as intimate and as close-up as we like.

To sum up, Lucy, as the object of all gazes, handles the narrative pressure accumulating on her body by latching onto a series of objects which in every case are figures of herself and in the final case is her very reflection. This only heightens the visibility of desire: all eyes on Lucy; her eyes on an object that throws her image back on herself. Without fear of hurting her we are free to look on, so hermetic is this image framed by the screen, masked by the lens, highlighted by the soft focus. The structure of the film, then, prompts us to revere the single, static representation and delivers Lillian Gish to us on an altar where she poses as a final value for us as for the Yellow Man. Instead of thrusting our gaze forward toward a narrative end, the film has displaced our drives in a delirious onanistic act of self-consuming sublimation. Art, conceived here as timeless, self-absorbed pictorial value, has used and transcended the "prop" of narrative to achieve this "higher" goal, this sublimity.

Griffith here instinctively attached himself to a conception of art meant to escape the crude self-serving Hollywood mold. Indeed sublimation, especially in art, was thought by Freud to be one of the directions the erotic drive might take in response to censorship.[6] It was the direction Freud implicitly felt to be most healthy, setting it up as he did against perversions like sadism and masochism. Griffith certainly believed that he was offering a healthy response to the eroticism of Hollywood and he treated his film as though it were the delicate frail Lucy whose beauty is hidden by blemishes (the poverty and haste of her production). Forced to live with and serve the musclemen of Hollywood distribution, she awaits an audience capable of appreciating her purity. Hemmed in by the greedy world of the entertainment business on one side and by the lusting "evil eyes" of the audience on the other, the film lowers its own eyes and cultivates its own beauty: it stares at itself, at Gish its center and central metaphor.

Gish's role and her style suggest the studied innocence of the child-prostitute, a standard Victorian character-type still titillating the sexual imagination of the post-WWI world. The

---

[6] Jean Laplanche and J.-B. Pontalis, *The Language of Psycho-Analysis*, trans. Donald Micholson-Smith (New York: W. W. Norton, 1973), pp. 432-33.

lowered eyes invite lascivious gazes. The lack of self-consciousness purifies the sexuality. Our response, like that of the Yellow Man, is to protect the girl from others whom she does not suspect desire to possess her, but it is also to protect her from her own self-knowledge. Her sexuality, like her beauty, is something rightly "hidden" from her, something only an artistic sensibility can bring to light without disturbing.

In protecting his film from Hollywood, Griffith must at first have been proud of himself, only later to have nagging doubts, for, despite its avowed otherness, *Broken Blossoms* was a film meant to compete with the average fare of Hollywood. It was a film that, despite its supposed innocence, would be deemed successful only when it had brought in money collected from patrons lusting for its promised pleasures, only in fact when it brought in more money than the more gaudy and straightforward streetwalking Hollywood films.

The marks of this doubt appear whenever the careful oppositions of *Broken Blossoms* collapse into equivalences. The sacred incense of the oriental temple has its counterpart in the mists of London. The pretty urchin of the Limehouse district makes us recall the three oriental maidens of the introduction. The missionary zealotry inspired by the temple's high priest and the text he reads to the Yellow Man is explicitly ironized by the British missionaries about to embark to China with their book on "Hell." The "spying one" can only be a British "evil eye," the opium den a fallen eastern holy place. Finally, of course, the aggressive erotic advances of Battling Burrows become the advances of the Yellow Man. He protects Lucy from the incestuous lust of her father out of another illegal lust of his own, the lust for miscegenation.

Unable to bear the knowledge of this equivalence, of the general human distribution of sexual desire, the Yellow Man and Griffith quickly turn that desire around upon themselves in the classic structure of reflexive masochism.[7] Under the sign

[7] Freud's consideration of masochism began already in the first of his *Three Essays on Sexuality* (1905), but the essay central to my concerns here is "The Economic Problem of Masochism" (1924).

of the Buddha and carried away by the incense of homage and self-intoxication, the Yellow Man, Griffith, and we the audience erase our baser feeling through a self-immolation made delicious and satisfying because of the distance of the love object. Lucy on the altar is the product of a gaze and in that sense is literally untouchable.

In the tradition of Tristan and Iseult and of Romeo and Juliet, Griffith thinks to reach the unattainable in death and self-sacrifice. The eternity of the rounded, androgynous Buddha is the model for the Yellow Man's inward curving posture, culminating in seppuku where he doubles himself over the knife to achieve an end to body and a permanence of spirit. Suicide is the mark of difference and the guardian of oppositions between West and East. Suicide differentiates the Yellow Man and his motives by forcing the final opposition, that between body and spirit.

The film, like the Yellow Man, destroys its western tendencies toward aggressive narrative action and direct involvement in spectacle, deriving pleasure from this self-proposed blockage. It seeks to attain the sublime through an interplay of narcissism and masochism,[8] providing another and more perverse reading of its images. For the submission of the ego to the cruel power of the superego even to the ultimate cruelty of suicide suggests, Freud speculates, the desire by the subject to attain a state of feminine passivity before an aggressive father.[9] Suicide is the final narcissism of the film, then, coming to double the death of Lucy, to find a higher equivalence in passive spirit outside all body and difference. But as Freud notes in concluding this same essay, "even the subject's destruction of himself cannot take place without libidinal satisfaction." Broken Blossoms is a film in search of back routes to this "erotic" satisfaction.

To begin, the bracketing shots of the ship entering the foggy

[8] The relation of sublimation to Narcissism is explicitly mentioned by Laplanche and Pontalis, Language of Psycho-Analysis, p. 433.

[9] Freud, "Economic Problem of Masochism."

harbor, shots, by the way, that remain completely unmotivated, create a *figure* for the slight narrative movement that
brings the Yellow Man back to his true spiritual home, towing
the audience to the threshold of a land that is at once new
and ancient. This land of China and eternity is the place beyond conflict, beyond difference, the place of maternal support. The story in turn elaborates a tale based on this image
of the ship returning to the motherland, for the Yellow Man
leaves the stable security of spiritual nourishment and embarks
on a life of separation, only to search for a final return to that
total buddhist presence.

The body of the film chronicles his descent from the temple
into the auto-eroticism of the opium den where the same
gestures of spiritual nourishment (marked by the incense) are
now performed for their secondary pleasures, as when the
child weaned from the mother finds pleasure in its thumb.
Then, in a classic recapitulation of narcissism, the Yellow Man
goes beyond himself by choosing for a love object someone
who is a replica of the image of his former self, the pure Lucy.
He buries himself in the ritual gown that robes her just as we
bury ourselves in the fetishizing close-ups of her face. This is
the desire for pure presence, for a cinema and an ethic beyond
or before the essentially sexual scenario of all narrative.

It is here that the equivalences between East and West, the
equivalence of all bodies and desires, disrobe the film's intentions, for this *is* a narrative film and it *does* display itself for
the pleasure of its audience. Caught out, the Yellow Man and
Griffith erotically disembowel themselves amid an incense which
expands their egos to the size of the cosmos. This is the height
of reflexive masochism, a melodramatic solution to the problem of sublimation. But it is an easy and facile solution, even
a predictable one, equivalent in its way to the vulgar attempts
at mysticism in Cecil B. De Mille's religious epics. It would
take Von Stroheim and Murnau to open up other, more healthy,
avenues for the *Art* of the American cinema.

CHAPTER THREE

The Turn and Return of *Sunrise*

D ESPITE the lapidary language we customarily employ to characterize them (as precious, brittle gems, priceless pearls), elasticity is the property of lasting works of art. It is perhaps their defining property. Not only do great works absorb the shocks and insults to which spectators put them year after year and century after century but their resiliency is in large measure their attraction for us. *Sunrise* is elastic enough to return to us intact after scores of conflicting interpretations have, over decades, pulled it this way and that. Indeed, our own interest in the film is held by its refusal to succumb completely to any one experience or interpretation of it. *Sunrise* demands reexperience because it "speaks back" to our first experience with an authority we can hardly resist considering autonomous.

Indeed, the very greatest works offer us a clear and satisfying experience only as a prelude to a demand for reexperience. As Paul Ricoeur has said,[1] their discourse conveys at once both a message and a "surplus" so that even the most carnal and ravishing encounter with the work's body spends neither us nor the work. We distance ourselves, survey our experience from on high, and feel compelled to return to that body. Its "surplus" protects the work from being devoured either in the flesh (by carnivorous experience) or in its image (by an Olympian and final critical view). A gravitational force,

This chapter was first published, in a slightly different form, in the *Quarterly Review of Film Studies* 2 (August 1977). Reprinted by permission of the editors.

[1] Paul Ricoeur, *Interpretation Theory: Discourse and the Surplus of Meaning* (Fort Worth: TCU Press, 1976).

this surplus allows for, and demands, a complex reaction to the work, one that draws us close but keeps us separate. Our reencounters with a work are merely repetitious if they refuse the offer of the surplus and fetishize one aspect of the work. But if we return to the work risking our first view of it, risking as well our view of ourselves, a dynamic is put into play that is oriented toward the future of the work and of ourselves. To be able to explain the *discourse* of a work of art is to seize its signification; that is, to seize it as a mark of something past and absent in a "regressive hermeneutics." But to respond to its *surplus* is to put comfortable explanations in jeopardy and to regard that mark as alive, as capable not simply of repeating its message but of ushering in new significance without warning, displacing its past, displacing our attachment to its meaning. A "progressive hermeneutics"[2] attends to this surplus striving for comprehension of self, of artwork, and of the shifting (elastic) process that forms their rapport. The tension between explanation and comprehension is the counterpart of the dialectic between criticism and experience, between our "placing" of the work and our "being placed" by the work.

Most film criticism has emphasized the repetitious nature of film viewing. Old-guard auteur and genre studies as well as vanguard psychological and ideological analyses all assume that ritual and obsession are at the basis of most cinematic creation and experience. Such criticism has few qualms about paring down a film to its "essential structure," reading the film as a symptom of a more fundamental obsession or state. Like any symptom, we attend to such films only long enough and in such a way as to read correctly the situations they indicate. In a mass art this seems appropriate.

But the film masterwork strikes us as far more than a symptom, and it demands to be heard again even after we have

[2] Paul Ricoeur, *Freud and Philosophy*, trans. Denis Savage (New Haven: Yale University Press, 1970), pp. 522-24.

traversed it and attained the meanings it seemed at first to symptomize. This is the reason for our sense of the autonomy of such a film, and this is the reason that explanatory analyses are appropriate but in no way exhaustive, for they stir up more questions than they answer.

THE fullest criticism of a film like *Sunrise* is a never ending one, a dialogue with the film that demands several "critical passes," each one qualifying its predecessor. We may well begin with a view of its relation to Murnau's themes and styles or with its particular evocation of the pastoral, the melodrama, or the medieval fable, but we will be forced to return to it again to go beyond these initial positionings of the film in an *oeuvre* and in a genre. These successive readings, suspicious or synthetic, develop a history of experience and of understanding so that the term "artwork" might better be thought of actively, as that which is done and changed, rather than passively, as an object to be weighed, measured, and catalogued.

The primary and overwhelming subject of *Sunrise* is self-consciously announced in the film's first titles: the bitter and the sweet, mixed in every life, are hailed as the timeless strains of a song celebrating the life of two humans. In a first passage through the film, *Sunrise* promises to deliver to us a concept, and observe for us the achievement, of humanity. The film's drama chronicles the movement toward this goal as a movement toward the bond of the couple.

This is a song of *two* humans and this two-ness is essential to the possibility of both song and humanness. Since the plot involves three characters, since Margaret Livingston received star billing along with Janet Gaynor and George O'Brien, this can only mean that she, the cat woman and vamp, is non-human, inhuman.

Just as this most natural of worlds refuses a song of three, so also is a solo inconceivable. The world of *Sunrise* is erotic at its base. Man needs woman and she him. Together they produce the song. The energy of the unattached human as it

searches for or neglects its mate is capable of wreaking inhuman suffering. The film traverses that suffering and promotes a discovery of the song of humanity as a ritual in which
the free sexuality of the individual is anchored by another
human. The naturalness of the sun beaming down its approval
on the couple at the end is not available to the individual.
When light floods the wife feeding her chickens earlier in the
film, its sanctifying glow is qualified by the mise-en-scène which
divides the outside from the inside [1], the left from the right,
making us recall the pathetic distance between her bed and
that of her husband; she is no Beatrice. Her achievement comes
only in relation to her husband as she is transformed from
the wounded bird of the café to the mothering bird of the
church [3, 4].

It is in the church that the couple is furthest from home,
yet it is here that they reachieve their union and validate the
family and community life behind them [27]. Before they begin
their voyage home (stepping out of the church to the approval
of a city community and marching toward and within a rear-
projected Edenic landscape), a beam of light delicately mottled
by an ornate window grid fixes itself upon them [4]. The film
will end when another such beam can transfigure them and
their home [32], but only after the man expiates the offense
that has driven them to the city and extirpates its cause. In
the church they bow before a higher law and are illuminated;
in the finale they become that law, become the sun, and illuminate the entire community. In John Donne's terms we
witness their "canonization": this is the community's song
about a pitiable couple who are not merely returned to the
welcoming community but whose return validates that community. From the outset, then, *Sunrise* is a purgatorial community ritual flowing from the screen to the spectator, who
is invited by the song into the ritual and into the community.
The first viewing of *Sunrise* is a complicit and integrating one.

W H A T is it that gnaws at the achievement of this canonization,
that makes us view this film askance? Surely it is the suspicion

that the community of 1927 America has cleverly designed
this "miracle" for its own aggrandizement and perpetuation.
The song of two humans becomes the song of nature, and
both not only are domesticated at the end but decree the law
under which domestication becomes a value. In this sleight of
hand the ideology of the average spectator undergoes a glor-
ification achieved by the very characters (the potentially universal Man and Woman) whose problems brought that ideology into question. Since their capitulation to the laws of
society (the laws of family) is pictured as the triumph of love
(eros and agape ringing out from the church bell tower) they
bring back from the church not only their determination to
live within the law, but a renewed grace, love, which is the
source of the law.

Thus, through experience innocence is regained, not only
the personal innocence conferred by forgiveness but a communal innocence that celebrates the origin of the laws of the
family and validates a posteriori the drama that questioned
those laws. As Mary Ann Doane has so forcefully shown, the
image of the sun serves to mask the contradictions in this
solution.

> The Man, in the beginning of the film, is tempted to
> test and transgress this law, but the law is re-invoked as
> supreme by the closure of the film. Furthermore, the man
> reassumes the place of the father within the family unit.
> The sun here serves to sanction and naturalize the Sym-
> bolic Order and the symbolic activity of the text. . . . Yet,
> the final signature of the text is not that sun which is the
> most natural thing in nature but an artificial stylized sun.
>
> The natural originary presence (of the sun), sanctioning
> the textual work and its symbolic activity, is always al-
> ready metaphorical—and everything, including nature,
> becomes Text.[3]

Our suspicion before *Sunrise* is certainly triggered and sustained by the inordinately powerful effect of the antisocial

[3] Mary Ann Doane, "Desire in *Sunrise*," *Film Reader* 2 (1977), 76.

elements which a first complicit viewing thinks to have suppressed. No doubt the marsh scene and the two frightening water journeys receive extraordinary elaboration precisely to increase the confidence of the community when they are dissolved like morning fog; but they also seem to have their own attraction. Here, of course, we are in the midst of the aesthetic of the horror tale, the mystery novel, the gothic romance. And here *Sunrise* could be, and has been, justly compared to Murnau's earlier work (especially *Nosferatu* and *Faust* but *Phantom* and *Schloss Vögelod* as well) and to filmmaking practice in the twenties generally. Indeed, it invites full-blown genre comparisons and those comparisons in turn demand an analysis of the social and psychological impulses behind this kind of story.

But rather than pursue investigations into such determining forces as William Fox's position in Hollywood, Hollywood's position in U.S. culture, Murnau's homosexuality, the decline of German expressionism, the function of the pastoral within recently urbanized societies, the problem of Christianity in a capitalist order and so on, all of which naturally arise here, I would like to emphasize the particular achievements of *Sunrise* in aestheticizing its problematic. While *Sunrise* is certainly another song validating the chaste life of the family while brutally banishing the sexual visions it couldn't help but entertain, while it is another compulsive version of a general myth, a symptom of a lasting psychosocial scene, the film continues to haunt us in its particularity. In our next return to the film we must not neglect its claims to universality which stem from its ideological work as allegory, but we must attend to the "progress" of this film in relation to its themes. For Murnau has reimagined this theme in a way that is new. While his problematic can be thought of as banal, powerful, ideologically complicit, eternal, or whatever, his film, as a visual meditation and interpretation of that problematic, permits us to make a gain, achieve a perspective, on its dark psychosocial origins, origins that will continue to fascinate us as they fascinated Murnau, who returned to this problem again and again.

THE surplus of meaning which overruns the banks of *Sunrise*'s traditional narrative is first of all a visual surplus. The precision of the compositions suggests a second text and a second context for meaning. And it suggests this immediately, for following the title cards announcing the narrative and thematic concerns of the film is a series of four autonomous shots grouped under the heading "Summertime—Vacation Time [5-8]." Under the aegis of this title and attributable to no source, these shots are able to establish a "look of the world" before that world becomes implicated in narrative. Thematically vacation time promises to test the values of a leisured class, but it suggests as well a visual variety based on free movement, free activities, and the boundlessness of a bright outdoors.

Narratively Murnau's four shots denote, in succession, "Good-bye to the City," "Vertiginous flight toward pleasure," "Relaxation," and "Welcome to the calmness of a new environment." But visually they form a much more pointed dialogue, a dialogue that continues through the remainder of the film. The first shot, a stylized painting of a train station, suddenly breaks into action as one train and then another pulls out of the screen. Shot 2 superimposes these trains on opposing diagonals in Eisensteinian conflict. Shot 3 is a split-screen vision of a stately ocean liner on the left which inherits the travel motif from the frantic trains, while on the right a woman in a bathing suit leans on a pier. From the bottom of the screen a man surfaces, nearly pulling himself up on the woman's legs. The final shot (actually three related shots) is classically composed by a camera that is inside a vacation boat as it nears a village shore. Two thin masts trisect the screen. Small sailboats run laterally across the top. Following an insert of the shore, the movement of the camera becomes autonomous as it cranes up for a full look at the village before descending toward the dock where onlookers are gathered to welcome it.

The shots establish four different graphic paradigms, and each of these paradigms will play a key role in the film's visual drama. The final shot of the prologue, with its intricate movement and perfect composition, might well be considered the most "typically Murnau" and it is with this that we begin.

A. Let us call its effect "classical," since it is in itself harmonious and geometrically proportional and because its simplicity allows us to read into it allusions to established graphic traditions. The passengers are arranged on the boat as in some early nineteenth-century French painting: the two thin masts trisect the screen like pillars in a quattrocento Annunciation [8]. The natural lines of movement in this composition are accentuated and complicated by two gentle motions: a sailboat breezily traverses the top of the frame right to left, and the camera lazily slides foward with the progress of the boat. Far from disrupting the composition, this movement seeks to rebalance the screen or to create a symmetry in time. In this case the camera gently leaps from the people on the boat, and, after surveying the village in its tame flight, comes to land on waiting onlookers and a waiting dock. Thus the moving camera independently seeks out the ideal (classical) point of rest, locking within the shot the energy that motivated it.

Much has been made of Murnau's virtuosity with camera movements, and those in *Sunrise* are breathtaking. Their power, however, largely stems from the spareness with which he employed this technique—only fourteen of over six hundred shots. Several of these are follow-shots in which the stationary camera decides to pursue the character in view. More accurately, the camera is pulled in the wake of a drama receding from it. The vamp early in the film walks by the panning camera and threatens to go completely out of view, but soon we are implicated in the cadence of her plan. Later, the man, back to us, wanders toward the marsh, and the camera, full of our desire, initiates one of the most complex and thrilling movements in all of cinema. It crosses the fence at its own spot, turns on the man who in his stupor passes by it and makes for the vamp. But the camera finds its own, more direct path, pushing past bushes until she is revealed in the moonlight. When the man reenters screen left we are doubly startled, having forgotten that we had abandoned him. Indeed, we are perhaps ashamed to have reached the vamp before him in our driving impatience. This shame is intensified at the end of the sequence when the camera, nose in mud, sniffs after the retreating sinners. It is a daring, highly unconventional shot, and it delivers its image of guilt not only by its content (high-heel shoes oozing with mud, while the marsh refuses to give up the imprint of the shoe), but by making us feel guilty as we literally track the couple down.

For the most part these tracking movements serve to animate and prolong classical compositions rather than manufacture drama. While it is true that most of the tracking shots, notably the trolley ride, open up new acting spaces for the marital drama, the very stateliness of the duration of these shots moves our attention from the drama to focus on the very design of the image. Indeed, the moving camera allows us to watch the shot in the process of being designed. This graphic rather than dramatic use of tracking contributes to the persistant view of Murnau as an "aesthetic," high-art director, a view reinforced by biographical attention placed on Murnau's study of art history and on the pictorialism of his earlier films, especially *Faust*. Scrutinized with the eyes of an art critic, *Sunrise* becomes an endless series of citations. Robin Wood[4] catalogues many of these: the still lifes of wooden bowls and bread on a table that is raked à la Van Gogh [9]; the second honeymoon voyage in which the vertical moon-streak and small sailboat on the dark lake recall paintings of the *Brucke* group; the scene of the search for the lost wife with its frontal image of bobbing lanterns, suggesting impressionism [17]; the inserts of the village itself [10], seen always mistily or at night with the steeple and full moon prominent above the clustered houses, which draw on a frequent *topos* in late nineteenth-century painting. I leave it to others to establish the sources for such "pictorially aware" compositions as those given us in the amusement park, café, or church.

4 Robin Wood, "Murnau II, *Sunrise*," *Film Comment* (May-June 1976), 10-12.

Wood goes on to suggest that the stylization of certain gestures is an even more important aspect of the heritage of painting in this film. The baby reaching to touch its mother's face [12]; the wife feeding her chickens [1]; the insert of the "holy" family under a fruit tree and beside the ox-drawn plow—one could multiply such scenes which suggest, which cry out for references. Frequently the drama itself is rendered as a conflict of pictorial styles. The delicately curved neck of the wife, whose head is consistently surrounded by a horizonless field of water, is juxtaposed with a frontal view of the man whose gesture of rowing thrusts him aggressively toward us. Indeed, the film as a whole has been seen as a conflict between expressionism and naturalism, Germany and America.

As in any fable, the story proceeds between two distinctly segregated poles: the vamp and the wife, the city and the country, land and water, night and morning. While the alternation of these elements produces a dramatic energy which is intensified by sequences of conflicting pictorial styles, the same energy can also be released within a single shot through the use of diagonal compositions, to which I now turn.

B. Conflict is explicit in the paradigm announced by the film's second shot—a locomotive screaming diagonally across the screen, crossed by another to form an X [6]. In the body of the film itself such energy is not so self-contained, for diagonals appear only one at a time and point to a space and a time beyond them.

Murnau saves this composition for a particular moment in the film, giving us a strong clue to the rhetorical strategy at work in his storyboard. After the wife has agreed to the journey and has said goodbye to her baby, we see the boat, the death ship, tied to the dock. Its diagonal composition is marked by the entrance of the man who draws the line with his heavy feet. There follows a sequence of some twenty-two shots before he and his wife are alone on the lake. Nearly all of these shots are self-consciously diagonal, a fact that gives unity to the sequence and allows for a silent drama between man,

woman, boat, and dog [13, 14]. Murnau would never allow
such compositions to achieve their own resolution but he does
let them build the growing tension. For instance, the direct
energy of the man is countered by that of the dog pulling
frantically at his chain to form an even purer diagonal. After
ten shots elaborating this graphic drama, Murnau shows us
the boat leaving the shore and, instead of cutting to the charg-
ing dog, he allows the dog to enter the scene from the center,
leap off the dock, and swim out to the boat.

A number of diagonals recur in the following sequences
until the boat reaches the farther shore. In the city itself they
are essentially absent. That they represent and contain a driving and perverse energy is attested to by their use in conjunction with the vamp. Particularly at the film's end she is
shown walking downscreen along roads or fence lines whose
diagonal composition leads her to the bottom corner of the
frame. Unforgettable is the scene in which she is driven by
the man diagonally to screen left and then rolled to the bottom
front of the screen by force of a fence which has cued the
direction of the action all along. Indeed, the vamp's final exit
from the village drops her diagonally away from us to the
upper left-hand corner of the screen, leaving the glistening
lake restored [31]. Murnau emphasizes the defeat of the diagonal when the shot following her exit displays the crossed
bodies of the reunited couple [15]. The diagonal is a figure of
absence as well as of passion; it is an image of a lack as well
as of the drive to fill that lack. In *Sunrise* it is overcome by
the presence of the cross which brings all energy back to a
center and holds it there.

The interplay between squarely composed images and unbalanced or diagonal ones, between the crossing trains and
the pleasure boat, dramatizes the narrative in a traditionally
pictorial manner. Murnau's achievement here lies in his ability
to make this interplay deeply conflicting without resorting to
conventional montage, and it is this for which we normally
salute him. Each shot has an integrity that makes it valuable

in itself. Placed in sequences these shots resonate even more fully because of the dramatic context in which they participate.

But such pictorial interplay is not unique to *Sunrise*. One finds it surely in Murnau's other works and in early German film generally. Moreover, Murnau isn't at all faithful in *Sunrise* to this strategy. The barbershop sequence, for instance, is a traditional Hollywood set piece complete with establishing shot and an elaboration of fragments. At one point eleven straight glances stitch the comic scene together, culminating in close-up inserts of the masher's shoe being stepped on and the husband's pocketknife slowly opening. What could have been a suspenseful scene is lightened in the overarticulation of its presentation. By rendering it via comic-strip montage, Murnau sets this fake drama off against the more primitive and powerful dangers which flank it and which he delivers to us intact, as if in awe of their permanence and seriousness.

The great moments of *Sunrise* certainly could not exist in montage. The evil and grace which this film imagines for us cannot be given fragmentarily nor could they be grouped and held within such logical and essentially human boundaries. The intelligence of the stylistic oppositions labeled here classical and dynamic is not congruent with these more supernatural aspects of the film. Through its occasional montage and through its consistently tasteful stylistic deployment *Sunrise* will always be recognized as a model film; but it is despite this taste and intelligence that *Sunrise* makes us return to it once more seeking the source of its more primitive attraction for us.

C. The first and third shots of the prologue provide entrees to another type of experience that *Sunrise* dares to envisage. If the frame and all its potentials for repose and dynamism can be seen as cultural modes of organizing conflict, these two shots suggest the film's openness to noncultural forces, to chaos and the preternatural.

Initially the third shot appears conventional enough, the two forces in the frame, an advancing ocean liner and a resting female bather, cut off from one another in split screen [7].

This shot in fact is the transition to the purely reposeful classical composition of the final prologue shot discussed above. It tames the dynamism of the crossing trains and, while maintaining the explicit conflict between two entities, it gives each entity an autonomous space within which to relax. Thus far the shot is interesting, even logical, but certainly not remarkable.

Suddenly a form disturbs this interplay. A figure rises from the bottom of the screen, a man pulling himself up to be with the woman. While his motion might be seen to counterbalance the descent of the ocean liner from the top left of the frame, something eerie far outweighs this formal explanation: we learn in this, the film's third shot, that *the frame is not sovereign*. We recognize that throughout the film it may be framing the wrong things or ignoring something hovering on its edges. Similarly the frame can drop elements once their dramatic importance is exhausted, exiling them from the play of light on the screen. The vamp suffers this fate when she is being strangled by the man [16]. His murderous intention is interrupted by the close-up of the nurse calling him back to the miracle of the rebirth of his wife and his hope. He lets go of the vamp who literally falls out of the frame, descending, we might imagine, to some other world. This is the opposite of the prologue shot where from the bottom of the frame emerged a sudden male presence. The vamp, we might further imagine, would have preferred strangulation. After all, he had tried to strangle her on the marsh before she was able to transform that passion into eroticism. But she is denied passion because she is, in the end, denied framing. She is lost to the world of the film and drops from it as though censored. She will, of course, be officially dispensed with in the film's coda in the shot already described as a diagonal leave-taking, but it is this moment of graphic rejection, this refusal of the screen to give her space, that is her true demise. For what lies beyond the frame? It is this question which *Sunrise* continually poses and which upsets all purely pictorial accounts of its power.

The power of the unseen and the unframed is attested to by every audience. The most startling moment of the film is invariably the sudden intrusion of a horse's head into the shot of the man hiding the bulrushes. This scene raises tension not because it is exceptionally dramatic, though it does bear with it the specter of the marsh scene, but because the sovereignty of the frame is shattered. If we are frightened with the man, for an instant our fear persists beyond his. For the fact is that we can no longer trust the framing of any shot. We must constantly run our eyes around the perimeter of the screen in search of the unknown.

Murnau first discovered this structure in *Nosferatu* when the mystery ship glides into the pretty harbor, disrupting its peaceful sleep and infesting it with plague. He returns to this very image on smaller scale in *Sunrise*. At the beginning and end of the murder voyage occur shots in which we see at first only a dock or a mooring post. Silently into the frame slips the shadow, then the prow of the rowboat. While the framing of these last shots is in part motivated by the function of a harbor, a dock, a mooring post, all of which exist to wait upon the arrival of a vessel, Murnau nonetheless could conceivably keep us waiting interminably in expectation of that which we cannot see. This sense of the interminable lies behind the most effective use of this compositional structure, the scenes of the search for the wife.

Lanterns bobbing from the prows of a huddle of rowboats create an effect Robin Wood termed "impressionist [17]." Like some Monet painting the function of the edges of the frame is very problematic. This scene with its complex molecular movement, its indecipherable composition, and its context of a black surrounding lake seems aimless. These boats go nowhere. These searching light beams cannot penetrate the lake below. The pathetic husband tests all perimeters. Once he even calls out along the frontal axis directly at us, the spectators. Is there any space that will yield up his wife? At the end of the sequence, in what is surely the film's most pathetic moment, his boat drifts and bobs completely out of frame. This moment of despair is achieved by the failure of cinematic framing, by the dispersal of the filmed elements in search of an absent center.

In the midst of these directionless shots Murnau inserts a privileged narrator's view of the wife floating unconscious [18]. This miraculous vision which no one sees begins on solid black. For four full seconds we are asked to stare at the imperturbable lake, an image of the husband's despair. Then a form grows in the upper right and begins slipping down the diagonal. The camera doesn't budge. It can't frame or even locate her. When she has completely disappeared bottom left we realize we are without bearings and that this inhuman accident of sight is over. The husband recovers a piece of lace, a trace of this passing, but the lake is black again. What we have been given here is a glance at grace. Its possibility has been affirmed as it has passed through our view, but its absence from the man and his drama has also been marked. Grace is as unframable as death. We glimpse only its trace.

It is in this same transcendental space, this time conjured up in flashback by the rescuer, that we view the miracle of the wife's recovery [19]. Once again a pitch black lake covers the screen, an undifferentiated chaos within which composition is meaningless. Then the rescue boat nudges in from bottom right and constructs the diagonal along which the wife begins to descend. The space of nothingness has been graced, yet remains imaginary, to be called to mind in memory or in story.

D. I have saved for last the first shot of the prologue, indeed of the film; for in its obvious internal mutation (from static drawing to live action), it introduces both the simplest and the most important paradigm of shots [5].

To begin with the simple, this shot announces a drama between expressionism and naturalism. The stylized flat of the train station with its latticework lines is animated without warning, great billows of smoke rising in the middle of the picture. As one train and then another moves out of the station, our eyes scan the screen for the realistic detail we had at first ignored in attending to the extraordinary design of the scene. One can hardly help watching for this kind of interplay throughout the film. Contemporary critics were alert to the contradictions Murnau's relocation in Hollywood was certain to elicit.[5] George O'Brien's heavy, hunched saunter plays against a sweet and airy Janet Gaynor, natural in the American way except for the East European wig all her fans bemoaned. More subtly, the peasant house which the vamp inhabits is European in decor and in presentation (the curiously raked table) [9, 10], whereas the final scene of the peasants is shot straight-on in American style. One is tempted to label all the dark scenes (marsh and both lake journeys) as German in their style, while the sunny sequences, particularly the middle portion of the film in the city, might be termed American. But this formula is too pat and fails to account for the graphics of the Luna Park and the café sequence. Nevertheless it may be true, as has been suggested, that this film is Murnau's final death struggle with the expressionism of his early films.[6] The expulsion of the vamp is then a clear victory for Janet Gaynor (her hair now luxuriously undone) and the American way.

Much more important than this obvious mixture of styles, the first shot of the film undergoes internal transmutation and it is this above all that characterizes Murnau's approach to action. Here a static design is magically animated. Later superimpositions will invade an image from within and corrupt or save it. Think of the lake bubbling over the face of George O'Brien, or the three faces of the vamp fading in from the space around O'Brien to tempt him on.

Referring to the darker German films of Murnau, Alexandre Astruc discussed the power of this method:

What will the image become? The meeting place for a certain number of lines of force whose placement will

[5] See Steve Lipkin, "*Sunrise: A Film Meets Its Public*," *Quarterly Review of Film Studies* 2 (August 1977), pp. 339-55.

[6] Mimi White, "Expressionist Tradition and the Project of *Sunrise*" (Seminar paper, The University of Iowa, 1976).

directly recall Velasquez and Caravaggio. Yet each image demands to be annihilated by the next tragedy which is installed right in the heart of the seemingly indifferent. Watch how corruption is born out of tranquility. Murnau operates slyly. The key to all Murnau's work is a fatality hidden behind the most harmless elements of the frame.

Each image is an unstable equilibrium, better still the distraction of a stable equilibrium brought about by its own elan.[7]

A perfectly framed and static view of the man's home is undone by a single movement, his shadow appearing in the window signaling the vamp [20]; or later in nearly the same situation, the shadow of his head by a small window preceding the sudden swinging open of the door [30]. These shots have something of the demonic about them as the composition disintegrates into a threatening action, threatening primarily because the mutation originates in the center of the frame.

Murnau carefully blocks his scenes to achieve this kind of effect. The crucial scene of the husband's return to his bedroom, sick with evil passion spent and with the onus of more evil deeds still to do, is given as an intrusion into the sanctuary of his wife's resting place. Small and unaware, she lies bathed in moonlight while from a downstage center doorway first his shadow and then his hulk looms up and covers her. Like the superimpositions of the vamp that finally urge him to take the awful step [21], to ask his wife to boat with him, there is no forewarning. In the center of a marital bedroom the specter appears. In the midst of life, temptation unaccountably wells up. Evil in the world of *Sunrise* cannot be warded off by vigilance. There are no boundaries to protect. It arises and corrupts from within.

So many shots reinforce this vision. Smoke and fog rise up from the center of dozens of seemingly static compositions. Murnau even used this structure in his intertitles when the

[7] Alexandre Astruc, "Fire and Ice," *Cahiers du Cinéma in English*, No. 1 (January 1966), 70.

graphics of "couldn't she get drowned?" [22] become liquid and slide iconically to the bottom of the screen, dissolving into a pictograph of the wife falling from a boat and in slow motion descending to the bottom of the lake and of the frame. Indeed the final image of the film is the resurrection of these graphics, "Finis" rises (as from the lake) to center screen and to a solidity that it has been the film's job to achieve.

Surely the most powerful use of this structure and one that speaks to us with an innate strength the years cannot diminish are the performances of the principals at those moments when we see an emotion or idea crossing their faces. Janet Gaynor stands before George O'Brien and his request that she come with him across the lake; she hesitates, her lips quivering, and then explodes into an unforgettable smile, certain that the long night of her husband's inner struggle is over [23, 24]. Characteristically, Murnau refuses to cut away from her to the reverse shot of O'Brien, for the drama must develop within the scene and in its own "rural" time.

Other privileged moments occur at the café as the man passes her the plate of cakes and her face disintegrates in tears. In the church it is O'Brien's turn to crumble and be restored in front of his partner. And of course at the film's end these two human faces beam together in transfigured joy only to demand further transcendental mutation: all within the immutable stillness of a perfectly composed frame these faces dissolve into and become the glorious superimposed sunrise. The energy of their love cannot push the film forward in time; instead it accumulates in the frame until it literally radiates its final image.

THE parabolic origin of *Sunrise* is unmistakable. The characters are nameless, their drama timeless. Its impact applies "wherever the sun rises, whether in city or country."

Who is presenting us this parable? Images, and paradigms of images, exist only as they are presented and become present to someone. Just as stories are more than a sequence of events, so images are more than an array of pictorial elements. What narration is to story, so framing is to images. Indeed the very term "to frame" is ambiguous enough to refer to representation and narration alike. We frame a picture and we frame a story. In motion pictures we frame both. And so, who is presenting us the parable of *Sunrise?* Early in the film we are shown. As the man leaves his home to pursue temptation in the marsh, we are given a sudden unaccountable explanatory insert. Two village women recall how "they used to be like children but now he ruins himself; moneylenders take their farm." These women conjure up the appropriate images to support their gossip and then one of them, whom we shall later recognize as the nurse, says, "while she sits alone." Her glance curiously seeks our own and for an instant we can be certain that the entire film is a community parable told by its citizens to us, an extension of that community. Thus the framing of the flashback to explain the story shows the visible presence of the storyteller and lets us infer the framing of the film as parable. In the film's final sequence the community once more explains to itself, and to us, the miracle of the rescue, taking credit for the happy end.

Between these two blatant interventions of community there exist many moments and types of framing, all of which put the images of the film to use. Think of the explicit dreams conjured up by one character for another: the image of the wife falling from the boat inserted by the vamp into the mind of the man so forcefully that it recurs even when he is alone; the pastoral garden in which the "remarried" couple takes their promenade; the angels with violins they dream up at the carnival; and so on.

This ability of characters in the film to situate or frame a scene leads to another graphic paradigm not mentioned above: *repoussoir.* When a character in foreground is silhouetted by the light stemming from a background scene, that character's thickness is lost but his or her control over the background scene is established. This paradigm is inaugurated in the film's first sequence when the vamp slips into the dining room of the home where she lodges. The peasants in the foreground

literally frame her entrance [9]. The next sequence opens with
a more dramatic instance of this effect. Two more peasants,
so sharply silhouetted as to be featureless, stand up against
the camera and to the right [25]. The vamp's exit from the
house throws the deepest plane of the frame into brightness
and focus so that we observe her, through these nameless
peasants, slink up the street. These two shots in fact prepare
us for the villagers' flashbacks to come. The drama of the film
is seen by and through the eyes of the village.

Other uses of *repoussoir* include the vision of the city seen
through the backs of the couple viewing it; the trolley trip to
the city in which the driver is flattened and darkened against
the bright landscape developing before him. The most complicated uses of this shot are reserved for the last third of the
film: the wife in a glance-object format eyes a couple dancing
at the amusement park. This couple is shot to look like paper
dolls pushed up against the dance-hall window. Behind them
the sparkling room appears full of other dancers and the band.
Since the camera begins to track in on this view we are in the
position of the wife framing a heavenly couple who in turn
sense the paradise behind them. Even more complicated is the
search for the adrift wife. Here the vamp frames the townspeople, first through her window and then catlike from the
tree branch above them while they in turn are silhouetted
against a further scene, the arena of the search itself [26].

These remarkable shots which explicitly pose the question
of seeing and conjuring are only the exposed side of a structure
that never ceases to operate in the film. *Sunrise* is an elaborate
interplay of viewers viewing and willful characters striving to
frame their desires. Nor are we as spectators aloof from this
interplay. We too have our desires and strive to frame this
parable for ourselves. When the vamp slinks down the street
she passes the village observers [25]. They lose interest, yet
we pan with her, we truck behind her, caught up in her lure
and in the mystery of her project. She stops to peer in the
window of a home where a man is having his hair cut. We
have voyeuristically caught her in her own voyeurism. Guilty

already, we track on to the fence of another house. She whistles at the little square of a window in front of her [20]. The
power of her whistle is part of her encompassing glance. Inside
the man at his table decenters the classic composition by leaning nearly off-screen in response. When she whistles again he
stands in the middle of the screen against a post. To his left
is the kitchen with his off-screen wife. To his right the off-
screen source of the alluring whistle. He is caught. It is enough
for Murnau to show us from the vamp's viewing spot the
shadow of a hand motioning in the window. The vamp has
made her conquest by commanding the field without being
seen.

In the famous tracking shot which discovers her under the
moonlight she prepares to be seen, but only as a necessary
tactic in her larger plan. She wants not to be taken but to
take. In the scene which follows it is she who controls the
frame from its center [11]. She grasps his head and glares at
us defiantly. She proposes the murder and keeps the man from
recoiling out of the frame. Right up against the edge he leans,
lifting his hands in horror. But he does not leave. And when
he throws the vamp to the ground she knows she will win.
Her final strategy is to point to the glories of the city. Sitting
before us, exactly replicating our own viewing situation, the
couple looks on at the marvelous vision unrolling before them,
a vision that inspires the vamp's voluptuous dance and the
man's aroused passion. It is "a movie" that has seduced him.
He gives himself to her. The actual moment of sexual inter-
course is signaled by a long shot of the moon beside the village
steeple.

The erotic iconography of this piece of censorship is unmistakable, but the shot serves to return the story to more
distant hands. The vamp who has controlled each frame to
this moment is relieved of the image in her frenzy. This is why
we must follow her tracks and locate her once more in the
succeeding shots. The steeple image has implicated the cosmos
itself in the sin and has allowed the vamp to step out of the
frame without losing her control over the man. Alone, he is

seen groping his way amidst the shadows of fishnets and
branches, still caught in his sin. It is only in sleep that her
spell is loosed, the water bubbling through his consciousness
like the river of Lethe, like the water into which he must send
his wife.[8]

The flowing dissolves carrying this water culminate in a
tableau of the village at dawn stretched out along the lake.
Murnau here has taken narrative authority from the man,
expressing thereby that relaxation of conscience the guilty seek
in unconsciousness. This momentary and illusory relief persists into the next shot as we reenter the room to find the wife
hovering solicitously over him, encompassing him in her self-
less gaze. The peacefulness of this transition is shortlived,
however, broken by the mad eyes of the waking man which
in delirium have mercilessly brought back in hallucination the
bundle of bulrushes he had so carefully shoved out of view.

This startling return of the film to his eyes is a burden on
the viewer who had only been too glad to be under the domestic care of his wife. Worse, the man turns his horror-laden
eyes on the wife herself and frames her as she feeds the chickens [1]. It seems at first that the power of her benevolence
richly described in this classically composed shot will be suf-
ficient to thwart his intentions. But as he looks at her, and as
he hesitates between the goodness he sees and the evil in his
eyes' intent, the lure of the vamp materializes in three superimpositions that hem him in [21]. Abruptly he stands and
walks into the image containing his wife, corrupting its purity
[2]. In this glance-object pattern we have been left holding
the glance while the viewer (the man) has entered the field he
had earlier framed. Thus we are made complicit.

The attempted murder can also be understood as the interplay between conflicting "views." The conflict is established
when first the man and then his wife sits alone in the boat
waiting for one another. A look of doubt crosses her eyes

[8] Dorothy Jones, "*Sunrise*: A Murnau Masterpiece," *Film Quarterly* 9
(Summer 1955), 238-62.

which now seek to hold on to the shore. Yet that shore rotates and recedes from her. The man is in control of the boat and of the horizon. She is under his view and looks frantically about at the shore she is no longer allowed to possess. As the crescendo nears she is continually framed against a solidly aquatic background that she can't escape. She looks left and right. A flock of birds flies away. There is nothing solid to hold her eyes. She slips under his power, cowering over the edge of the boat, falling into that background, until her hands reaching out in supplication break through the trance of his intention. He falls back and rows to the shore. At this point Murnau once more relieves his couple of the drama. Neither character can look at the other. Both relinquish the scene. Murnau cuts freely around the boat, letting the energy of the oars and the thrusting prow carry the film to the shore.

The second movement of the film, the reconciliation in the city, absolutely alters the direction of the first. Where before we had an interplay of wills, now we have a convergence of wills. Where before we participated in the flight of desire, now we participate in the desire for stasis.

The entire city section is cushioned in protective brackets that insure its harmony. The trolley, which leads the disconsolate couple in, later takes them happily away. Twice the wife is protected from the treacherous traffic: once blinded by despair, once by euphoria. Twice the couple find themselves in restaurants, once unable to eat or look at one another, they must leave; later they eat and look so much that they fly away in imagination. Between all this narrative protection and framing lie the great images of reconciliation for which the film is well known, the scenes in the church and in the photographer's studio.

The reconciliation in the church, after the failure of flowers and cakes, is attributable no doubt to God and his visible presence in the lighting of the mise-en-scène. But more powerfully, it is a product of art, of a mediated experience that allows both parties to mingle their feelings at a protective distance. The spectacle of the wedding depersonalizes the power of love so that it can bypass the horrendous breach of promise represented in the film's first movement. Where personal love failed (cake and flowers), institutional love succeeds. The unworthy find worth beneath the umbrella of the church's blessing, a blessing general enough to extend beyond the sanctuary and into the congregation [27].

In positioning themselves before this ritual the couple asks anonymously for the blessing. They view in order to be renewed. By reason of their anonymity the couple here implicates the audience once and for all. The gaze of the spectator in the back row is bound up in the gaze of the man at the ritual before him. His identification with the groom and its power to bring him to his knees keys our own identification with the man. The film here signals the mode of response it demands from us, signals itself as a ritual, the very observing of which has the power to liberate the viewer. Having looked at this spectacle the man no longer needs to look at his wife. He buries his head in her lap and she bends her neck in protection. This pietistic moment closes the distance between them so that their glances no longer need to meet or avert themselves. They look now together at a future that opens up before them, thanks to the mediation of a spectacle engrossing enough to command both their views, meaningful enough to unite them.

If the sequence in the church places the spectator within the process of narration, the photographer catches that same spectator in the act of imaging. The couple themselves demand a final framing in which the world looks at them, in which they lose their sight and become sighted. Their kiss, inverted in the lens, captured and held on the photographic plate, is the culmination of their reconciliation. It is this physical object, this icon, which rests cushioned between the frames and brackets of the city section [28].

The pleasure the photographer takes in framing them, a pleasure mutiplied by all those who watch their country dance at the carnival, is of course entirely too facile. The anarchic impulse of adultery is not so easily tamed. The dance and the

photograph embody a social solution (an artistic solution) to
a problem society only pretends to control. The photograph
and the dance, like Murnau's classical compositions, pretend
to hold and objectify a social value, but these values themselves can be seen within a larger, nonsocial context. This
shifting of contexts produces the film's most beautiful moment. As they sail home under a benevolent honeyed moon,
the couple in foreground "images" a barge of dancing peasants
floating across the top of the frame [29]. This scene brings
into nature the dance of the amusement park, and it explicitly
rhymes with the vision of the city framed earlier by the vamp.
Like that earlier vision and like the wedding spectacle viewed
in the church, the image of the barge produces immediate
consequences for the viewers. The couple reaches together in
their one explicit moment of mutual sexual interest. But the
barge floats off the screen, and its irridescent bonfire gives
way to the surrounding blackness of the lake. The family unit
is blessed by society in the photograph and in the serenading
barge; but both blessings are suddenly nothing more than little
squares within a larger more forbidding frame.

In this context, the wind preceding the storm is unframed
and unframable. Driving the city dwellers out of their artificial
pleasures, it leaves the floating couple without social support.
Nature's passion, indiscriminately unleashed in this storm,
threatens the simple reconciliation of the city. Passion and the
vamp demand to be heard.

The fairy-tale quality of this cosmic justice is supported by
the shift of the film to the view once more of the vamp. Bare
skin gleaming in the intermittent light, she glares at the townspeople first through her window and then from her tree [26].
At the height of the drama we are presented with the film's
most complicated visual moments. We frame the vamp who
in glance-object format frames the townspeople on the shore;
they themselves are staring into the darkness of the lake at
little rescue boats. The men aboard those boats look in despair
at the forlorn husband whose eyes frame the blackness of the
water. At the center of this intricately embedded structure is

the wife's absence. At the outside stand we, the film spectators who, with the vamp, observe the pathetic impotence of society in the face of this absence.

The final drama to be played pits the dominant gaze of the demonic vamp against that of the man. Having looked into the nothingness of the water, he returns to the sanctuary of his marital bedroom and kneels before the empty tabernacle of his wife's bed. He ought, it seems, to give up sight and life right here, but he is awakened from his emptiness by the whistle of the vamp come back to envelop him. Her error is to enter the space she has framed. Whereas before he had gone to her, now she goes to him, invading the sanctity of the house [30].

Murnau achieves an enormously satisfying shift of power by letting us watch, from her imperious post behind the fence, the foolish audacity of the vamp. Instead of commanding the scene from that post, this time she inserts herself into the scene. The terror of the storm, the night, and the dark side of passion are condensed in her small form which hesitates outside the house. In chasing her down and brutally burying her beneath the frame, the husband clears the way for refilling the house. The all-seeing vamp has been seen; passion has been recognized and dealt with. Domestic life can now be sanctified by nature itself [32]: the entire family, seen all together for the first time since the pastoral flashback, arranges itself on the wife's bed. The cross of her window frame, instead of throwing its portentous shadow, is now wreathed with flowers. This unmistakable Easter icon is motivated only by the resurrection of a wholesome love through the near death of the innocent wife, who suffered to redeem the sinful husband thereby casting Satan back to hell.

This ending satisfies the on-screen community. Outside the couple's room they recount the rescue. And then, as if to laugh at the fate just overcome, they reenact comically the origin of the story: the rescuer accepts a kiss, two kisses from the nurse, and his wife tweaks him by the ear. This little flirtation once more traces the cracks in the social structure, cracks it was the work of this film to caulk. It recalls other "light" moments like the man's attack on the barbershop masher, like the comic flirtation of the vamplike manicurist, and like the sudden violence of the woman with the falling shoulder straps. Together these jokes dismiss with laughter the paradox of sexuality as the basis for marriage as well as for adultery. The community's solution to this paradox was to freeze the couple in a second wedding ceremony, in a picture, and in a dance. Yet these social solutions are put in jeopardy not only by the storm but by every antisocial gesture society tries to cover with laughter.

And so the unenlightened community retires with their laughter and leaves us alone with the couple. As we have seen, the diagonals generated by the drama here at last cross themselves in stasis. Here the easy "look" captured by the photographer and tested by the desperate "looking" in the night is transformed into the source of all seeing, the sun. And here finally the framing of people and desires which has propelled the film from image to image can end: for we are confronted with a tableau that looks back at us and holds us prisoner beneath it. When the projection bulb goes out and the houselights fade in, we sit staring at a screen that has lost its glow. The almighty sun, able to hold the very image of love, was itself a prisoner of the screen. And as we look about, the film becomes once more a parable, a snapshot of love, at sea in a more pervasive darkness. We are ushered out of the theater like the community from the couple's home.

Like all great art Sunrise has given us an impossible image, the timeless satisfaction of our yearnings, a limitless "looking become look," a "conscious sun." The recognition of the impossibility of this yearning is the final achievement of the film or, more properly, of the experience of the film. The couple has escaped the rising and setting of the sun by becoming the sun. We mortals must watch it pass out of sight aware of our distance from it and from them. The experience of Sunrise, then, is an exercise of our sense of distance and of light, of framing a world and yet being at the mercy of that which is beyond the frame.

VISUAL life is an oscillation between searching and being positioned. In *Sunrise* this oscillation is explicit, and we have used the dialectic "framing–being framed" to describe it, but we might as easily have talked about surfaces and depths. For to hold an object or a person in view is to pin it to the screen and to treat it two-dimensionally [28]. Whereas, to be at the mercy of an unstable frame or of a scene (the wife adrift [18]) that resists framing is to experience the solidity of that which we seek.

This opposition between framing and being framed is at the heart of cinema. In its determination to create good stories and beautiful tableaux, cinema tries to hold the world in its power. In its failure to do this, in the nonnarrative, unpainterly aspects which form the grain of every film and become foregrounded in some, cinema is at the mercy of what it strives to perceive. This opposition of surfaces and depths speaks explicitly to the viewer of the film, for it marks a tension in the movie theater. On the one hand the spectator joins the community and "uses" the example of the story to recover and reinvest a commitment to culture. The film is like a mural painting on which the viewer can see the couple, the community, the locales of danger, and even himself, and across which a world view is reframed. On the other hand this same spectator has paid an admission fee to leave social positioning behind and to dream alone in the theater whatever dreams the film might evoke. A voyeur concealed before a fascinating spectacle he does not control, that spectator wants in part to be caught out, framed suddenly by a turning of the light on him.

The very phenomenon of cinema, it seems, feeds these conflicting impulses. As social critics insist, movies are the plaything of the dominant ideology. They are, even in their pretenses at social comment (pretenses *Sunrise* at least has the good taste to ignore), thoroughly institutional products supporting an institutionalized way of life. Yet movies are also considered dream material capable of appealing to and unleashing our most nonsocial fantasies.

It is *Sunrise*'s feat to have paid tribute to both these impulses in its narrative structure, in the interplay of its graphics and, most stunningly, in its implication of the viewer within its flow. Watching it, we are led to agree with the nurse that there is a moral order in the universe and that it has generated our culture. But we can also sense the mystery of events beyond the nurse, beyond the community. The primordial chaos of the vamp and the inhuman beauty of the apotheosis of the couple let us imagine a life beyond social health and prosperity. And in our imagining the film repositions us, decentering us from our social selves. It is no doubt this tension between the positioning we perform on the story and that other positioning it performs on us that makes us return to this film again and again.

The experience of *Sunrise* is in the mode of the experience of any masterwork. Its story is as conventional and ideological as renaissance *topoi* like the Nativity or the Flight to Egypt. Its craftsmanship, like the flawless form of a fifteenth-century classic, seems unquestioned and unquestionable. It puts the eye and the mind to rest. But as classic, *Sunrise* assumes the aura of the institutions with which it is complicit; it is after all a product made under the patronage of William Fox. Fox bought Murnau and his German expressionist team explicitly to construct for him a piece of high art. This mogul of the "low-class film" commanded the creation of an artwork to rise loftily like a dirigible over his studio as advertisement and as example.[9]

No doubt the Medicis had better taste than William Fox, but they served in their day a similar function: to foster work that would at once advance the art and uphold the culture, drawing special attention to its patron. Such works deserve their homes in the Uffizi at Florence or the Venetian Accadèmia, or the National Gallery in Washington, D.C., places whose location and architecture assure our proper respect.

[9] Robert C. Allen, "William Fox Presents *Sunrise*," *Quarterly Review of Film Studies* 2 (August 1977), 327-38.

The thousands of viewers who file up to such works, like those thousands in our classes and film societies who are placed before *Sunrise*, are placed before a cultural monument. The stability and "correctness" of the story and the form assure their respect and perhaps their admiration. The very structure of these works likewise insists on a certain positioning of the spectator called for by the use of perspective and, in *Sunrise*, by the narrative. Hence the spectator not only fixes a world but is fixed in relation to that world. This is the hidden and insidious task of every classic: under the guise of greatness and even of freedom, supported by a philanthropic patron, artists advance the institution of art for the glory of culture. The artist's product becomes an artifact of prestige and of the market, capable of being owned, sold, used as collateral. And collateral it genuinely is, for it guarantees the social order that produced it! Moreover, as a classic it is displayed pedagogically to instruct all members of a culture in the rightness of that culture and in the reposeful attitude they should assume before an order that is both vast and natural.

But *Sunrise* is more than a classic, and it is on this surplus that we must end. When Giotto shaped his *Flight to Egypt* he did not disturb the story nor did he disrupt its visual form, creating as he did a much-imitated composition. This is Giotto's classicism; but his faces go beyond such good taste and sense. They have mystified and disturbed for centuries and they will continue to do so. They mark a dimension of his painting which cannot be accommodated to an institution and which cannot be easily "placed" by a spectator. Indeed, they unsettle the spectator in a depositioning that requires a reappraisal of the work, if only to permit that befuddled viewer to regain balance. Similarly Piero de Cosimi's Medici-sponsored allegories disorient us by the distention of his figures and Filippino Lippi's by the strange radiance of his colors. This radiance doesn't *serve* the monumental aspect of his painting; it *disturbs* it, haunting the spectator in the process.

In the same way *Sunrise* can disturb and disorient even while it recounts a myth, even while its form puts us at ease. In the eerie, unpredictable power of the frame, and in the even less predictable transference of the work of framing, *Sunrise* continues to unsettle. We admire its surface to be startled by its depth.

If this is the potential of all cinema, it is the realization of a very few works indeed. And if we sense something beyond respect and admiration for this film we must find a new word for our experience: awe. *Sunrise* partakes of the awesome. And it insists that we return to it, not in blind obsessive reenactment but in a deepening comprehension of both work and self insured by the oscillation of positioning and unbalance we undergo. If this film is a masterwork, its mastery is something that changes hands. Ultimately we master this film only to find ourselves mastered in return.

CHAPTER FOUR

The Fever of an Infectious Film:
L'Atalante and the
Aesthetics of Spontaneity

Y ES, the academy legitimizes many of our obsessions, allowing us to relish in public what we enjoy in secret, and the cinema is the latest instance of this psychosocial economy. But not every sort of discourse about film is culturally acceptable and not every sort of movie is admissible.

There are two basic types of academic film criticism, a sociological approach and a humanistic one. The movies can be studied as consumable products of a particular cultural appetite, the analyst situating him/herself in a position of power above the work and reading it in relation to some aspect of culture such as history, psychology, ideology.

Alternatively, a film can be considered part of a canon of valuable artistic forms and can be scrutinized as a locus of traditional aesthetic concern. The humanist treats certain great films as displacements of the religious and aesthetic values that formerly animated painting, the drama, stained glass, and the like. In this case the analyst is situated beneath the work, revering its particularity, interrogating it for answers to great human questions or admiring its expression of unanswerable problems.

In this context L'Atalante must be a scandal to the academy. Unpopular in its own brief day, it can scarcely appeal to the sociologist. Unpretentious, unpolished, and seemingly trivial in subject matter, it thumbs its nose at the humanist who is embarrassed to admit it to the canon. L'Atalante is a film kept alive by cinephiles who applaud it for its distinctively cinematic merits. They have been pleased that the industry of academic criticism has had such difficulty with the film and that its exuberant creator, Jean Vigo, patron of ciné-clubs, has so obstinately resisted induction into the accepted cultural mausoleum of "artistic geniuses." To talk of *L'Atalante* one must open up a third mode of discourse which, on the strength of its subject, may challenge in an important way the usual languages of analysis and of appreciation that dominate discussion of film.

FRANÇOIS TRUFFAUT, the greatest cinephile of them all, initiated in August 1959 a contest for all *Cahiers du Cinéma* readers, offering a prize for the best essay bearing the title "La Fièvre de Jean Vigo." This was in fact the title of an essay he had promised Eric Rohmer, editor of *Cahiers*, but found himself unable to deliver because of his new obligations as director and producer.

Philippe d'Hugues won the contest and his appreciation of Vigo was published in the October 1959 issue.[1] It pleased Truffaut no doubt because of its forthrightly unapologetic tone. Although Vigo died at twenty-nine, just before the premiere of *L'Atalante* in 1934, although his films total less than three hours running time, although together they cost less than a single one-minute Anacin spot to make, although they contain frequent lapses in continuity, technique, and execution, and a general lack of polish, d'Hugues tells us that we must neither patronize nor fawn over the man and his output.

D'Hugues writes, "Vigo's works aren't youthful if one means by that certain mistaken directions, a lack of maturity, or an incomplete vision of life. What earlier critics took for error is for us a good part of the price his films demanded." This price has another name, that of the title of the essay. It is a metaphor

---

[1] Philippe d'Hugues, "La Fièvre de Jean Vigo," *Cahiers du Cinéma*, No. 101 (October 1959), 25. Truffaut did write an essay on Vigo's work and did incorporate the metaphor of his "fever," but this essay (dated 1970) was only published in his collected writings, *The Films of My Life*, trans. L. Mayhew (New York: Simon and Shuster, 1978), pp. 23-28.

that literally destroyed Vigo while giving life to his films, "the fever of poetry in life."

The poetry of *L'Atalante* is, before anything else, sheer feverish perception: the too-clear and quivering eye of the camera darting about, selecting this or that, forcing relationships among perceived objects and forms. This is d'Hugues's "fever of poetry in life," and it attracts us because it doesn't clear away all obstacles at the outset but challenges reality with its own intensity. Vigo permits the heterogeneity of objects, situations, and feelings to disrupt the story while he joins them through the nearly hysterical gaze of his camera. Indeed, such random heterogeneity is a precondition and a mark of his fever: objects crammed on the screen, or tossed on-screen (cats); the insufficiency of conventional framing or of individual shots to cover the action, producing exceptional shifts in angle, scale, and light; optical deformations seeking to make visible various levels of perception (the fog [3], the hallucination [12], the night of "spotted longing" [13, 14]); and, most often noted, the multiple roles played by objects and by actors. Michel Simon as Jules embodies "pluri-signi-fication" through his various guises (gruff, affectionate, beastly, kind, commanding, tractable, childlike, ancient) but even more through the rapidity of his changes of guise. At Juliette's sewing machine [4] he is quickly by turns more domestic than she, docilely dumped over by her push, getting up to do a Cossack dance, then to fight a bull, then to model a skirt. The narrative can't hope to enclose either this character or this actor; he is a signifier of the excess of life over history and as such a condition for Vigo's excessive and feverish narration.

While *L'Atalante* has captured the affection of all but its first audiences through such energy and spontaneity, it is a settled as well as an exuberant work. Its unexpected bursts of plotless action (Jules' impulsive haircut, his Greco-Roman wrestling) and its wild shifts in pictorial scale and angle are buckled within an overarching narrative, a localizable time and place, and, most important, a clear rhetorical schema of motifs and symbols. Primarily these structures provide a dramatic base for brilliant moments of acting, or picturing, but they develop an undeniable power all their own as well. We realize this forcefully as we assent to the logic of the film's ending, abrupt though it be. The reconciliation of Jean and Juliette aboard the barge is effected not by a mechanism of plotting but by a strict use of parallel editing, for which the motif of the bridge is directly symbolic. The bridges the barge passes under, the bridge Jules crosses in search of Juliette, and the bridging melodies of Jaubert's musical score lace the fragments of this film together in a final flourish of moral and dramatic satisfaction [9, 10, 15].

These fragments owe everything to the clusters of motifs to which they belong, so that we accept the propriety of the ending as that of a coda, each shot bringing back into play some charged value established earlier on. Jules crosses a bridge, follows an unidentified woman to a cheap hotel, then bumps fortuitously into the loudspeaker horn on the street, hears the sailor's ditty coming from the "Palais des Chansons," and thereby discovers Juliette. This sequence makes sense to us because of our having seen Juliette forlorn on a bridge, stalked by ominous men, retiring to a cheap hotel, and because Jules has stolen a Victrola horn and heard that ditty before. Similarly Vigo can forgo both dialogue and significant glances in the final reconciliation between Jean and Juliette by returning to earlier motifs: Jean shaves in a bowl in which he "can see his love" and then wrestles Juliette to the floor, Greco-Roman style. The swiftness of this moment is in keeping with the tone of the film and avoids the triteness Vigo so loathed in the script.[2] Further, it permits the ultimate aerial view of the barge nestled between the shores of the river, enclosing its own happy couple [16]. Our applause as the film ends is reserved not for the characters but for Vigo, who has so deftly charged, then orchestrated the values that the film displays.

[2] P. E. Salles-Gomes, *Jean Vigo* (Berkeley and Los Angeles: University of California Press, 1971), p. 151. Salles-Gomes' biography, which originally appeared in French (Les Editions de Seuil, 1957), is the source for most later discussion of the making of this film.

All in all, then, Vigo's method is far more sober and calculating than has ever been thought. True, his use of his materials seems boundless in scope and energy, but he remains
faithful to a limited quantity of materials. He is obscenely
inventive, but never promiscuous. He restricts his characters
to four or five, his locations to a barge and Paris. His props
are no doubt bizarre, but they are easily enumerated and
grouped. All this invites us to imagine everything we see in
the most metaphoric ways possible. Vigo does not canvass the
world to cram into the film whatever suits his fancy. He stares
intensely at a pregiven world in order to imagine what is not
at all pregiven.

The viewer and critic alike must quickly catalogue the film's
obsessions. To begin, the barge itself is both domestic and
economic, a houseboat and a vehicle of trade. It is a means
of escape for Juliette before becoming her prison. Almost an-
thropomorphized, it needs to be steered by Jean (a superego)
while holding in its depths the hidden memories, fantasies,
and baggage of Jules' libidinal cabin. At once male and female,
it thrusts its way through the water while protecting the family
in its warm belly. Vigo is at pains to photograph this barge
at all times of the day and in all weather. The incomparably
beautiful entrance to the Parisian locks, for instance, places
the barge (up to now the entire geographical field of the drama)
within a larger geographic system, Paris, whose magical name
had come to Juliette over the radio.

On board Vigo has insisted on certain animate and inani-
mate props. The omnipresent cats, symbols of, and goads to,
sexuality, scratch both Jean and Juliette, multiply on the wedding bed, express the confusion Jean feels by running over
broken dishes, and serve as Jules' pets. Soon we find Jean
stalking Juliette [2] on all fours and Jules flipping about the
deck in animal fashion.

Jules' room is itself a treasure chest of symbolic objects.
Some are multisensory like the seashell Juliette listens to and
caresses, the tusk she strokes, the fan whose design suddenly
fills the screen, the delicate music boxes Jules turns [6]. Others

are outrageously phallic, particularly the puppet conductor who rises grotesquely into the frame as the music quickens and then falls forward, spent [5]. Jules sits behind this toy, which boundlessly amazes Juliette. Most memorable, of course, are the pickled hands [8], culmination of a series of remarks about, and shots of, hands ("These objects are all handmade," "These hands have done such things," Jules slicing his hand for Juliette, or pretending to strangle her earlier on the sewing stool).

A different sort of symbolic cluster is formed by the mechanical musical instruments which Vigo scattered through the film. Doubtless these delighted Jaubert who was obsessed with what I must call the "physicality of music" and who happily lets us hear the scratches in Jules' old phonograph records and the sound of air rushing through his cheap accordian. The pedlar makes us appreciate the bodily effort involved in producing even the crudest music during his solo on the quay, and Juliette marvels at the powers of the radio even though it transmits more static than signal. We even see patrons paying to dance to an early jukebox and to listen privately through earphones to tinny parodies of melody at the "Palais des Chansons."

The built-in opposition in this musical cluster between the physical and the transcendent reminds us that all clusters work by oppositional interplay: the barge is set against the shore, morning against night, the country village against Paris, the limitless sky on deck against the clutter below. We have male versus female, the civilized versus the primitive, and on and on. Two master symbols balance these oppositions: those of music and of the river, music that both calms and excites, is physical and transcendent, and the river that reflects from its surface but contains in its depths, but that in all cases, and especially in the last case, flows on reassuringly.

This type of symbolic logic operating through clusters and their opposition is common to some extent to all films. What distinguishes *L'Atalante* is Vigo's instinct to use such relationships to extend rather than delimit the connotations of his objects, characters, and motifs. Locked into a scenario not of his choosing, Vigo uses the story thrust upon him to explore the outer reaches of every element that story brings up.

"There's a story behind every object," Jules says, and in this spirit Vigo films. His attempts at evoking the latent or unexpected qualities in his decor and actors is fabled. If the cold air made breathing visible, he would invent a vigorous action to spread the breath of his actors around the frame. If nature cooperated with a fog, he would have his cameraman Boris Kaufman amplify the effect with yellow smoke and with sharp beams of light to cut through it [3]. The filming of the snow scenes in Paris is legendary. Vigo caught the sad line of the actually unemployed not to insist on the documentary character of his intentions, nor even to save money and time, but because it looked perfect and he knew he could push it to signify the threatening otherness of Paris.

If individual tableaux were insufficient, he would invest small sequences with the unexpected and the excessive. When Juliette has her purse stolen we are given two preview shots of the thief. This makes all poor male figures appear threatening, and it humanizes the thief, modeling his frail body wasted by cold and hunger. The nightmare of his chase is rendered by the darkness of the shots and the slatted fence through which we must watch it. In a characteristic pattern Vigo starts to terminate the sequence by showing Juliette watch the capture of the thief, only to pan over to a decrepit and patently lecherous old man panting as he moves toward her. The fear and disgust generated by the drama is instantly multiplied by this non-narrative icon of evil at her hem. Thus the quiver that goes through her is a quiver at the general notion of evil, a physical revulsion produced by evil's pure image rather than by a drama with malevolent consequences.

Similarly, in Jules' room Juliette turns away from her intense bodily sense of Jules and his bleeding hand to find him a bandage. But the experience of Jules is one of excess and Vigo won't allow her so easily to cope. A cat hurtles in from screen right and claws her breast. Once again a narrative (the knife, the cut, the will to heal) is multiplied by a non-narrative image and gesture, a cat at the breast. The suddenness of both these assaults on Dita Parlo, who played Juliette, undoubtedly kept her off her guard and gave Vigo the opportunity to catch certain spontaneous reactions. But the timing here also signifies, in its own right, the limitless imagery of the world ready to come into play if given the slightest pretext. The cat and the old man are condensations and thus appropriately excessive in relation to the narrative and even in relation to the vignettes to which they owe their existence. Condensations, symbols, metaphors . . . their method is to erupt from the story world of the barge and Paris and to express instantaneously the situation that the narrative has developed in logic and leisure.

The tension between story and image is apparent even in the opening moments of *L'Atalante*, where a struggle develops between narrative space and screen space. Generally first sequences of narrative films are clear and expository, setting the terms of the drama in a carefully delineated time and space; but *L'Atalante*'s beginning is thoroughly dislocating. It is impossible to place the church in relation to the town and both in relation to the canal. Performing a calisthenics of editing, Vigo plays with every border of the frame, with huge changes in scale, angle, and lighting, all at the expense of the episode he is depicting.

We can attribute the lack of proportion in the images to a childlike narration, the effect of which is to rivet our attention to the visible since we cannot depend on the smooth unrolling of a story and its world. Vigo capitalizes on this attention and rewards it at certain moments by constructing visual figures that are at once exquisite and very readable. When Juliette boards the barge on the boom (Vigo, we are told, improvised this when he discovered the gangplank missing on location) Jules pushes her screen left. Just as she passes the frame-line, Vigo has her reenter left and swing right past the camera and onto the deck. This illogical and startling shift of direction is easily taken as a visual correlate of the break she is making with her past, with the shore and its comic community.

Another more conventional function for Vigo's abrasive angles and cutting is to create dramatic tension. The mating struggle which opens the next phase of the film seethes with uncertainty and wildness not only because of the incredible contrast in costuming (a wedding dress rumpled by greasy overalls [1]) but because of two strategic infractions of the "180-degree rule."[3] Jean is first on Juliette's left, then on her right, then again on her left. We forgive these errors, assuming that Vigo is trying to provide, amidst the clutter on deck, the optimal vantage point from which to see the deflowering of a virgin. But the abrupt changes in screen direction serve to emblemize this moment and to drive Juliette from the frame completely. Then follows her unforgettable wedding march on deck: the counter-motion of the water, another barge, and a steaming locomotive, sets off the blazing white dress high-lighted by a traveling key light against a dusk that is still photographically deep. Vigo's harmonious visual rhythms here join Jaubert's wistful theme as balm to sooth the cat's scratches on Jean's face and the 180-degree slashes in the scenic space.

So far we have accounted for Vigo's narratively impover-ished and visually rich technique by trying to incorporate it in a larger view of narration, specifically as figural discourse commenting on the action (the parting) or mimicking its un-conscious side (the fear of deflowering). Vigo's search for odd angles and odder liaisons between shots is, however, more pervasive than these limited figural instances. We must, I think, face up to his interest in the sheer aesthetics of the image, in visual tensions and releases which play in conjunction with, but do not in most instances directly amplify, the drama. The film searches for a means to represent in a frame the longing, the separation, and the troubled coexistence at the heart

---

[3] For this analysis I am indebted to Mimi White's paper on the first eighty shots of *L'Atalante*, "Jean Vigo and the Space of Desire." This paper was written for Jacques Aumont at Le Centre Americain du Cinéma et de la Critique in Paris in 1977.

of the tale. This visual search frequently obscures and even breaks down the logic of narrative, troubling every ambitious reading of the film.

Because of the triteness of the narrative and the insufficiency of its presentation, because the surface of the film is marked over with strong discursive slashes, because the fever of the narration, in sum, is forcing something "more" out of every image, the film can only be read as an address to the spectator, more direct and vivid than we are used to or comfortable with. In this way our imaginations (and those of the characters) are invited to go beyond the story to the possibilities of the physical world within which that story takes place and thus finally to return imagination to perception so that, in Truffaut's words, "this dense daydream can lead us constantly back to reality."[4]

THE paradox of L'Atalante should now be clear: to the degree that it disregards and even thwarts its own narrative development by means of a strong, independent concern for the formal qualities of cinematic representation, to this degree L'Atalante seems able to express a dimension of life closed to most fiction films, precisely because their hermetic narrative structures use, rather than explore, appearances. This paradox must trouble the critic who wants to classify the film among the classics, yet who finds the notion of "classic" assaulted here by its lapses in standard cinematic practice and by its nearly improper appeal to the spectator. Nor can the critic readily adopt the common option of classifying this film "avant-garde." True, Vigo was never a disciplined narrative filmmaker. His roots surely lie in the Parisian and Russian avant-garde of the twenties supported by a radical social vision inherited from his celebrated anarchist father.[5] Yet while it is

[4] François Truffaut, *Films of My Life*, p. 28.

[5] Salles-Gomes, *Jean Vigo*, chap. 2. The many books and articles written on Vigo all depend on the biographical information Salles-Gomes unearthed. The interested reader, however, might also consult Marcel Martin, "Jean Vigo," *Anthologie du Cinéma*, vol. 2 (Paris: L'Avant-Scène du Cinéma, 1967), pp. 349-408.

useful to compare the constructivist impulse of *L'Atalante* to the aesthetics of surrealist automatic writing, of action painting, of the primitive films of Cohl and Jasset, and of the experimental films of Clair and Buñuel, Vigo's techniques do not operate in isolation from the film's love story. Although the story was thrust upon him and although he adapted it in one desperate night, chopping up its horizontal flow to give it vertical density, Vigo abandoned neither the tale nor its spirit.

And so it is wrongheaded to applaud the film for subverting its subject, or for promising more than it delivers, as if its mistakes point to an ideal text that only a lack of health, time, and money kept Vigo from sculpting. This would involve us in a most Platonic or Crocean conception of the artwork. Nor must we search in the clutter of the finished product for the spirit that generated it, peering through the film to catch a glimpse of Vigo's irrepressible personality. No, the film demands to be valued in itself, as a tale whose rough-hewn and experimental quality is integral to its achievement. Vigo's directness of presentation insists on this.

Not content to embellish a story we might read safely and in our own fashion, he blares his tale like a musical instrument whose sounds radiate immediately to us. The "errors" we sense in the presentation are the sounds of Vigo's nearly bodily effort to reach certain notes or to force his story to deliver up sounds it is hardly capable of. He performs his story, eyeing the audience all the while. And what of us, the audience? Such a performance may excite or embarrass us, but in any case it makes a direct appeal to us. From this point of view *L'Atalante*, like all of Vigo's films, is not to be understood or even followed so much as palpably felt.

Vigo had not only an aptitude but also a sure instinct for sensory manipulation. Bazin called him "the most deliciously obscene of directors"[6] no doubt for his unmistakable obsession with the flesh of his actors but also, and more subtly, for

[6] André Bazin, "Jean Vigo," *Cahiers du Cinéma*, No. 26 (August-September 1953), 63. This quote is also cited by Truffaut, *Films of My Life*, p. 28.

his concern with the textures of sounds and images. This
concern is most notable when Vigo harmonizes disparate textures to produce in us a kind of synaesthesia. On arriving in
Paris, Juliette climbs up onto the deck. She emerges into blind-
ing sunlight just as the barge's bell clangs. The light, the clang,
the squinting of her eyes, the spontaneous smile signify serially
that a new stage of life is to begin for Juliette, but far more
important they strike us simultaneously as a multisensory shock
that leaves our fingers tingling. Vigo approaches all the possibilities of the medium with attention to their physical effects
first, their meaning second. This is why his collaboration with
Maurice Jaubert proved so singularly successful. Before creating melody, music is the vibrations of materials and of air.
We never forget this in *L'Atalante*.

In any survey of types of sensual images in the film, by far
the most memorable belong to the sense of touch. Vigo tries
to overcome the distance of our eye from the screen in the
most inventive ways. Why else fill the film with cats? They
attack Jean and Juliette and make us feel their claws, yet they
ask to be stroked. The litter on the bed and in the linen closet
keeps the visual image alive with pulsating animal flesh.

Next comes Vigo's obsession with hands and with tactile
symbols: Juliette's seashell at the ear, the nude picture patted
by Jules, the stroking of the tusk, the opening of the fan, the
sliced hand, the pickled hands, the combing of Jules' bristly
hair, his tattooed body, and the manual energy of his accordion playing all involve our own sense of touch. If this were
not enough, Juliette becomes a surrogate spectator when her
tongue automatically responds to Jules' cut in a gesture of
attraction and repulsion [7]. Just as on her wedding night her
sexual desire had been kindled at the sight of Jean's cat scratches,
so now she seems to want to lick the old man's wound. As
difficult as it is to watch flesh sliced by a knife (recall *Un
Chien Andalou*, Vigo's favorite film, a blatant unmediated
sensory assault on its audience) we find ourselves salivating
with Juliette.

Throughout this scene, seeing and hearing are all invitations to touch. This is why, despite whatever our feelings for Père Jules may be, he can only be seen here as seducer, showing Juliette his collection of bizarre things, playing sounds for her that will invite her to touch and be touched. The entire cabin soon appears to us as a chamber of sensations. A nearly continuous camera take caresses each surface in close-up, permitting us little breathing room, little visual and rational distance, and blending all forms and objects within an atmosphere so close one can nearly smell it.

Vigo was not beyond playing unashamedly, pornographically on our senses as in the insomnia scene during which the longing of Jean and Juliette is not only amplified through Jaubert's most intoxicating orchestration and through matched editing which creates in a mental space the dance of two bodies in lovemaking, but the images of each character have been heightened by sexual fever until unmotivated spots polka-dot the screen [13,14]. Recently Boris Kaufman wondered if he went beyond the bounds of good taste in trying to swell, by means of a spontaneous improvisation, what was already the film's most obscenely tactile moment.[7] Here we can see and appreciate the creative effort while we enjoy its effects, in the same way that a jazz pianist's sudden hammering or foot-stamping at the height of his performance amplifies the effect of his magic while drawing attention to him, the magician.

VIGO'S impulse to pornography, to the direct sensory manipulation and gratification of his spectators, is redeemed by the narrative he tells, not by its logic so much as by the position it assigns us as spectators. Involved though our bodies may be in the sheer unrolling of sounds and images, we nonetheless are schooled to watch in a disciplined way the building and release of a drama. Earlier we placed the ethos of this film somewhere between that of the avant-garde's immediate re-

---

[7] Boris Kaufman, interview conducted by Donald Crafton in New York, January 1978. The transcript of this interview was made available to me by Professor Crafton.

lation to the viewer's perception and that of the classic cinema's highly mediated relation. The particular "voice" of *L'Atalante* asks that we entertain its story while responding to its flights. We need to be taught to adopt this ambivalent position in front of the screen and Vigo has not failed to provide us with teachers: Jean and Juliette.

In a very real sense this married but troubled couple embodies the dual urges we spectators have for the known and unknown. Like Jean we seek to possess the good image, to make it submit to our pleasure. We expect it to be untainted, virgin, and to gratify our senses while not troubling our lives. We want a stable representation, enclosed and enclosing, useful and harmlessly beautiful. We want to domesticate the film, to appreciate it, show it off (if we are critics), and re-enjoy it whenever we care to.

But simultaneously we seek with Juliette the promise of the unknown, the excitement of some action capable of taking us, filling us, remaking us. The trepidation and eagerness at play on Juliette's face and on her nerves as she leaves her home for a life "at sea" are models for our relation to this film as well. Open to something outside ourselves, cautiously putting ourselves in the hands of a helmsman we only half trust, we peer out, not at the helmsman but at the world that his journey (now our journey) allows us to explore.

The first third of the film is dominated by Jean's authority and his desire. As spectators we are only too ready to accommodate him in his passion to frame and possess Juliette. Even the hesitancies of that first night's love ritual on deck with its approaches and parries [1], its violent scratches and soothing promenades, seem timed to heighten our desire through calculated and reasonable delay and not to thwart or detour it. Jaubert's score relieves all doubts; its theme announces in its first notes (when Juliette is joined on the prow by Jean) a direction that can only end in the satisfaction of our ears and desires. Vigo celebrates this narrative and sexual achievement in a scene the following morning when the three men serenade the blushing maid, Jean crawling like a cat [2] over the camera to tickle our spines with his whispers of love in her ear. Vigo can scarcely cut away from the pleasure filling her face.

It is only as they dock in Paris that Vigo encourages us to neglect Jean's world in favor of Juliette's. While he is off pulling the barge to shore, Juliette comes alive to the exotic aura emanating from Père Jules. This is the film's most important development: the emergence of Jules as the character of beauty and mystery, displacing Juliette as the primary object of our gaze. Although he appeared first on screen, beating an impious yet superstitious retreat from the church, his presence in the film up to the sewing machine sequence is mainly decorative; that is, he is treated as are the cats, the cabin boy, the barge itself, as part of the bizarre new home to which Jean has brought his bride.

It is his performance before Juliette on and about the sewing machine that captivates her imagination and that of the cameraman as well. At his favorite angle ten feet above the action, Boris Kaufman has framed the scene like a cage for this frisky animal. Reaction shots of Juliette reverse her role so that suddenly we find the need to go beyond her as image of *our* desire to confront Jules, the image of *her* desire.

The actual confrontation takes place shortly after in his room, a psychoanalytic space of memory and fetish, where we stand alongside the amazed Juliette framing no longer her clear face but the direction of her amazement. We see her but we also see past her to Jules and his history. There we are immersed in an ocean of "otherness" until Jean breaks into the room and into the frame to reassert the legal, rational, and primary order.

He drives Jules out of the cabin in a disruptive act that pits our two desires in explicit opposition (our desire, and Jean's, for Juliette, the good image, narrative logic and control versus our other desire, Juliette's, to pursue and submit to the unknown, to Jules). Through no overt action of his own, Jules has broken the traditional dominance of man over wife, of story over image. A third term, he gives Juliette the opportunity and the need to plot her own life and seek her own image. Reciprocally Jean loses the command of the story and even gives up the helm of his ship. Henceforth he lives on the conjurings of imagination, his own feeble one in the water, his mate's strong imagination at the helm.

Jean, Jules, and Juliette (the integrated society, the integrated psyche) are dispersed in Paris and will only be reconciled magically at the film's end. For Juliette accepts the invitation she sensed in Jules' room to escape the latticework frame Jean had built around her, to be pulled into a dance by a traveling pedlar, and to try her own story, to "imagine" herself elsewhere and otherwise.

In Paris Juliette finds her image. It is compressed in a single shot on a store window, reflected beside brightly lit baubles [11]. The most formal picture in the film, it is, in both subject and treatment, an image of pure narcissism: Juliette delighted to see herself, Vigo aglow with the independent beauty of light and geometry. This is the culmination of the search for exotic images which, from the film's opening sequence, has been a perpetual if marginal project.

With this fulfillment of Vigo's formal tendencies and Juliette's exotic wishes, the film risks halting in self-absorption. But the pleasure she feels with herself and her bright world framed before her is soon contaminated when she realizes that she is prey to other lookers. Her lovely image in the window lures raincoated men to her body before that window. Our own presence, as more distant lookers still, becomes insidious.

L'Atalante is a dream, nightmarish and erotic, of a virgin before marriage. Jean has stolen Juliette from the law of her family only to impose on her another law. Her rebellion against the strictures of a scenario written to enclose her, has led her to Jules, to the pedlar, and finally to Paris. But Paris is not a refuge from tyranny, for she has suspended the order of Jean's plot only to discover the threat of countless other plots which implicate and abuse her, the visible plots of small-time thieves and lechers sidling up to her, the unseen plots responsible for the lines of the unemployed, for fleabag hotels, for every sort of exploitation she is subject to.

While Juliette, an image without context, is helpless in Paris, so Jean is helpless on the barge, a floating tale without value. In his desperate plunge into the canal Jean unites himself to her image in a pure hallucination [12]. The visual satisfaction of this representation (like that of Juliette before the window) is complete, but as the film continues to unroll, we as spectators are confronted by the hollowness, or rather the two-dimensionality of such perfect pictures. Indeed the very fullness of these representations (their self-conscious purity) marks them all the more as mere representations, and bespeaks the fleshly absence of their subjects.

Here we have reached the center of Vigo's preoccupations: the primacy of flesh within the necessity of representation. The film's most luxurious scene makes this explicit. Distracted with longing, the lovesick couple prepares to sleep, each alone in a narrow bed. Simultaneously they conjure up images of one another's bodies. Under the surge of a single musical theme, and under the net of Kaufman's blotchy grid, the lonely masturbation of this sundered couple is socialized, aestheticized, and redeemed until it becomes one of cinema's greatest expressions of happy oblivious lovemaking [13, 14]. Absence has become presence by means of the entirely cinematic processes of lighting, editing, and music.

The paradox of *L'Atalante* is that *presence* can only be fulfilled in a process that begins with *representation*. Jean thinks he has made Juliette present to him by pulling her on board his barge and he marks her presence by sticking his head in the bucket, saying, "I can't see you." "You'll see me when you really need to," replies Juliette. The plot of the film exists only to manipulate Jean until, in despair, he does indeed call upon her representation in the water of the canal. When she returns bodily at the end it is in a full presence which his "image" of a wife at the opening could in no way encompass.

The optimism of this film couldn't be greater. Jean's new conception of his wife is a new conception of society, one guided by the spirit of Père Jules. It is he who rescues Jean from the clutches of one evil boss and Juliette from those of another [15]. He brings them together to form a new community based on collective harmony, respect for the mystery and spontaneity of each member, yet fidelity to the group project of life together.

Jules the id-figure has become the grandfather of this community, engineering its success before returning to his elected subservience. It is he, not Jean nor Juliette, who is our final tutor, teaching us how to watch this film and how to live our life. For of all the characters, Jules most fully knows the use of representations in the projects history brings us. Surrounded by the mementos of his past, living a life rich in superstition (the play of cards, the sign of the cross, the fear of the broken mirror) he has even turned his body into a screen of tattoos which "keep [him] warm." The sound of the sea in his shell, the ditties of his musical toys, the accordion he plays, and the Victrola he is forever tinkering with vibrate the air around him and fill his atmosphere with the rhythms of life as it might be led. The character closest to symbols is, through symbols, literally in touch with life.

And what of us? Jules schools us to go beyond the one-way dreams with which we began, dreams on the one hand of control and on the other of anarchy. He would have us watch this film in the same way he listens to his Victrola, seeing it as a clumsy physical mechanism magically capable of producing melody. This is an age-old insight, that the artifice of poetry may attune us to the experience of life; Vigo has given us not merely this insight but its dramatic realization. L'Atalante is a powerful representation whose forthrightness demands that we go beyond representation. It is a film which by means of the sheer physicality of its expression invites us to attend to the sights, sounds, and actions of the things and people around us. It is not so much the film we celebrate as the vision of a film coming into existence, not so much a transcendent song as the pulse of sounds in rhythm, not so much a final harmony as an authentic representation of what community might feel like.

If the film charms rather than preaches, it is because for

Vigo, as for Père Jules, there is nothing transcendent about art or morality. These are not achievements so much as instincts, instincts, it is true, that civilization has lost, but instincts all the same. Catlike, Père Jules is the film's most artful and moral being, his sensuality a guarantee of his authenticity. The same rhythm of life, the same fever that drives the cats, drives Jules, Vigo, and each spectator not yet immunized against it.

CHAPTER FIVE

Productive Discord in the System:
Hollywood *Meets John Doe*

MILLIONS watch each year when Hollywood bestows its Academy awards, genuflecting before the ideals of art. This moment confirms its ordained episcopal role: worthy or unworthy, Hollywood, like the Church, claims to be the mediator through which its members may attain the sanctity of art and, in doing so, guarantee the rightness of a universal hierarchy headed on this earth by the leaders of studios and distribution companies. No recitation of its alleged misdeeds, of its spreading secular dominion, of the crass behavior of its potentates, can contaminate the grace that flows through it to its devotees. Hollywood has never pretended to be virtuous, except in this: that its cruelty and bad faith, its greed and its groveling, have created a versatile culture industry in which genius may achieve the pure and spiritual goals of art.

The film artist in Hollywood has always been treated as the favored son of a ruthless industrialist. Off at the best finishing schools, he knows little of the murky origins of the family fortune. The sins committed in the quest for power are to be expiated by this innocent Siegfried. When a conflict does arise, when the hegemony of power is at stake, it is always the son who must capitulate or, in the usual gesture of defiance, leave. Murnau must have felt this as he set sail with Robert Flaherty for pristine Polynesia, and Welles when in disgust he fled to Europe in search of patrons who knew something about the care and fostering of genius.

But how can we say that Hollywood has ever been unin-

This chapter was first published, in a slightly different form, in *Enclitic* 5 and 6 (Fall and Spring 1982). Reprinted by permission of the editors.

terested in art? How can we forget Welles' glorious invitation
to RKO, where he was given "the most expensive electric
train" any adult had ever toyed with, sheerly on the promise
of genius he had displayed? Murnau, too, came to Hollywood
under a million-dollar contract because William Fox was so
eager to upgrade and sanctify his enterprise. In that era Hollywood plundered European film talent without thought of
cost. This is hardly the neglect of art.

But the cinematic art celebrated each spring in Southern
California is popular art, not the pure marginal discourse of
aliens like Murnau and Welles. For the cinema that has been
touted as the art of our century is precisely the cinema of
genres and mass taste, not the cinema that contorts itself into
the postures of painting or poetry.

From this point of view, the men and women whom Hollywood beatifies are not at all those pampered children, re-
ferred to above, who have been kept far from the filth of the
factory, but instead those children brought up to move into
the firm, eventually to run it. The difference they make, the
energy they bring, is not the excess of rebellion, obtuseness,
or effete obsession. It is the productive difference that all
capitalism feeds on, especially in this industry, where novelty
is a chief value of the product sold.

Such novelty has most often been attributed to the "craft"
of studio personnel or at best to their "artistry." But the
tension between the institutional norm and each ambitious
film emerging from the system is precisely the tension we
recognize in the case of the lone genius who struggles against
the system. And so it should hardly surprise us when, from
time to time, Hollywood personnel, the sons of the industry,
adopt the inflated vocabulary of art in parrying the stifling
rules of their powerful parents.

In all events, by now few retain the image of the classic
Hollywood cinema as a vast undifferentiated mass of mindless
filmmaking. Tension and experiment are part of this era as
they are in every period of every cultural institution. Naturally
the Hollywood machine systematizes individuality and today

forthrightly markets it. But even in the heyday of the system
when Hollywood was proud of its image as "dream factory,"
the counterdreams of the great *auteurs* must not be seen as
altogether separate from Hollywood but as bound up with
Hollywood in a single, though variable network of links and
causes.

In this context Frank Capra must emerge as a figure worthy
of continued study. The system's most consistently successful
practitioner, he was immensely proud of the general popularity of his films, not to mention the incredible salary that
popularity permitted him to accept without qualms. He was
Mr. Hollywood, the man who directed its greatest stars: Jimmy
Stewart, Gary Cooper, Jean Arthur, Barbara Stanwyck, Clark
Gable. Yet Capra never tried to disappear behind the system
as, say, Mervyn Leroy or Michael Curtiz seem to have done.
He was "the name above the title" who knew, better than
any of his peers, how to use the system.

There is reason to entertain his claim to a kind of moral
distinctiveness, for after his fame had given him a sense of
personal strength, he immediately hoped to separate himself
somewhat from the system that had reared him in order to
speak with a still more personal voice. In 1939 Capra began
his adventures as an independent producer. Admittedly his
primary goal was financial. He hated to see Columbia Pictures
picking off the best fruits of his effort and his talent. Yet he
was also genuinely anxious to get away from the prying pa-
ternal eyes of executive producers. Why should he have to
bargain for script ideas or for personnel? Why couldn't he
now choose his own projects and his collaborators in the
French manner, since he had earned this independence by
rising to the top of the system? Why couldn't he begin speaking
directly his own ideas with his own voice? The mere fact of
financial independence gave him a sense of moral rectitude.

It is, I think, crucial that Capra saw his first independent
production *Meet John Doe* as a chance to prove to both the
system and to the critics and intellectuals on the edge of the

system that he was a man of conscience, insight, and intelligence. He himself said:

> No it wasn't the existence of critics that really riled me. It was their supercilious attitude that got under my skin. I had made seven smash hits in a row. Had I performed that feat on Broadway I would have been canonized. . . . As it was, not one of my last three films—*Lost Horizon, You Can't Take It With You,* and *Mr. Smith Goes to Washington*—had made the New York Critics Annual Poll of their selected "ten best" films.
>
> So I can truthfully say that it was the box office customers who made Frank Capra whatever he was or is. I was not invited into motion pictures, nor did I enjoy special favor of finance, nepotism or critical influence. I simply did my thing with films and the people responded. And yet, an ego like mine needed—nay required—the plaudits of sophisticated criticism. The Capra-Corn bards had pierced the outer bubble.
>
> And so *Meet John Doe*, my first completely independent venture, was aimed at winning critical praises. Riskin and I would astonish the critics with contemporary realities. We would give them a brutal story that would make Ben Hecht sound like Edgar Guest.[1]

The film did indeed make the critics sit up. It was lavishly praised. More important to Capra, his peers in the industry applauded his daring. David Selznick said that this film made him "proud to be in pictures."[2]

What Selznick and the critics seemed to like was the direct presentation of a conflict between good and evil in which the outcome wasn't clear. The age was ugly: Hitler in Europe, fascists in America made hatred and evil representable concepts. In *Meet John Doe* these bitter representations "hit a

---

[1] This and later citations concerning the film's production history come from Frank Capra, *The Name Above the Title* (New York: Macmillan, 1971), p. 297.

[2] *Ibid.,* p. 305.

standoff" with Capra's good folk, discoloring the limpid moral
solutions his populist films had advanced. "My spirit and
those of the audience would now have to seek a solution."

Meet John Doe was self-consciously ambitious in its aspi-
rations. Capra conceived it as a personal film, a film that
would address Hollywood from a position of independence,
a film that would address the crisis of the depression and the
lure of fascism. He wanted to speak with an authentic voice.
If the film is less pleasurable than *Mr. Smith* or *Lost Horizon*,
it was due, he felt, to the truth of what he had to say.

This was the "other side of the Pollyanna Capra." Instead
of the small town virtues flowing like mountain streams through
the corrupt city to purify it (as in *Mr. Deeds*, for instance, or
Mr. Smith), now we find the big city mentality pushing across
the country. Indeed, the politics in the villages is already seen
as corrupt. Even the heroic little man has lost his innocence.
Gary Cooper as John Doe is very nearly a moral cipher, a
tabula rasa waiting to be used for good or evil. More disturbing, the John Does of the world can achieve morality only
in nonpolitical social union, yet in 1940 it was clear that such
moral power as the people may attain on their own could be
quickly corralled and, in a single stroke, used by political
forces. Because of Germany, it was not a matter of more or
less politics. Politics was inevitable and in Capra's world inev-
itably bad.

The contradiction here was insurmountable. People alone
are amoral, together they achieve morality, but as soon as
that togetherness is organized politically they become im-
moral. This was something Capra believed: it was systema-
tization that killed the best impulses in human beings.

At the very moment of *Meet John Doe* Capra was organizing his huge Hobby Shop in Los Angeles according to these
precepts. It was to be a building full of work areas and sup-
plies. His hope was that, by allowing craftsmen who were out
of work to tinker free and at their leisure, new inventions
would bubble up. All patents would be held by the Hobby
Shop and one-half the proceeds from them would be plowed

back into the operations of an ever expanding Santa's workshop. Capra's partner in this naive scheme was Howard Hughes who was to supply most of the money, Capra contributing the spirit. Like all naive schemes it went under at the first collision with reality. Ironically, in this case it was *Meet John Doe*, a film about the little people, that killed Capra's real-life hope for aiding those people. Capra claims it was Hitler and Hirohito who subverted his venture. He blamed them as well for siphoning warmth and optimism from his film. He even suggested that the *era* was responsible for his failure to come up with a natural ending to his film.

Capra saw the relation of film to history as direct and immediate. If his films were dark and murky, it was because this was the tone of politics throughout the world in 1940; this was also the tone of Hollywood, or so Capra felt as he struggled to gain his independence. Not only would *Meet John Doe* carry the tone of the times, it would explicitly dramatize the problems facing the average John Doe in the world and the individualist in Hollywood.

While not an allegory in the strict sense, *Meet John Doe* nevertheless turns on the opposition between power structures and the little man, mediated by the technocrats of the press whose job has much in common with Capra's own. When Barbara Stanwyck loses her position in the opening sequence [1, 2], it is because of a command from the top which is insensitive to her talents and needs. Her ability not only to survive in this milieu, but to thrive and, in some respects, master that milieu expresses Capra's sense of his own accomplishments in the cutthroat Hollywood system.

Typically, Capra poses the opposition between power and the everyday citizen as dramatically as possible; most interesting for us is the fact that it is posed directly in relation to questions of media and of persuasion. On the one hand we have D. B. Norton's vast telecommunications network, with its broadcast station and its newspaper. The man of politics speaks via the voice of technology, amplified beyond all reasonable proportion, drowning out counterstatement. On the other side, the ideas of the ordinary citizen express themselves through intimacy and personal contact: Barbara Stanwyck in the silence of the night draws inspiration from her father's diary, at once the most homespun and most trustworthy of media; the soda jerk calls over the hedge to old "sourpuss," leading to the house-to-house personal organization of the John Doe Clubs; finally, the power of an embrace and even of the threat of suicide is the ultimate authentic means of persuasion in which the body itself becomes the means of communication.

While Capra evidently fights so that intimacy might conquer technology, presence conquer absence, what kind of medium does his own discourse represent? What form of communication and persuasion is *Meet John Doe*? In serving as his own executive producer and personally taking charge of nearly every aspect of the film, Capra surely felt he could sustain in his film the aura of personal presence symbolized by the father's diary. Naively, Capra could only believe that if the individual is pure, then his ventures or statements can be trusted if the organization by which he states them is independent; thus anything confused or disorienting in such statements must be the product of some outside force, usually politics.

But this is nonsense. First of all, Capra's so-called independent company was not only linked to Hollywood through every element and member of its production, it was indeed the apotheosis of Hollywood. From 1937 on big producers and directors were finding it lucrative to break with the studio contract system in setting up independent companies, *Gone With the Wind* being the most famous example. In other words, Capra was at the forefront of the economic history of a changing but very healthy Hollywood system. Secondly and most importantly, the movies are not a means of expression so much as an apparatus expressing itself. Capra could say only what this apparatus permitted him to say. No one believed in this apparatus more than Capra. All his films speak the language of Hollywood and necessarily represent its values.

Meet John Doe is no exception to Hollywood. After all, it is an explicit reworking of Capra's earlier films. Its complication develops as a mixture of genres, particularly the newspaper film and the Warner's hobo film. The system, rather than Capra's spirit, dictated the direction and look of the picture. His inability to end the film in a satisfying way testifies to this. Showing it to numerous preview audiences, he tried no less than five endings hoping to find one that worked. Obviously it was convention, not Capra, that would dictate what worked and thus what would be said. Even his vocabulary betrays this homage to the filmic apparatus. "Why did hundreds of scenes integrate into a jigsaw puzzle that had greatness written all over it except for one gaping hole no last scene could plug up?"[3]

Meet John Doe, like all Capra's films, is indeed a jigsaw puzzle: hundreds of pieces fitting cleverly and nearly seamlessly together to present a single clear picture. This is the method of the classic Hollywood film, a method employing a rigorous and restricted set of techniques all aimed at suppressing interest in the fragment (in the sound or image) to further interest in the story. Not only are the stories drawn from conventional genres and subjects with a rhythm of exposition, conflict, complication, and resolution; but the story is presented in the clearest possible light. The entire apparatus of the cinema is brought to bear simply to clarify character relations and plot progression. This means framing characters and lighting them to bring out their importance, miking them to allow human dialogue to overcome natural sounds, using background music to key audience sympathies, maintaining consistent light and noise levels even when this means tampering with profilmic situations, using camera movement to focus interest, match-cutting on action to hide shot changes, setting up internal visual relations through glance-glance or glance-object cutting [1, 2] and through close-up inserts which organize the world around the characters, and employing vis-

[3] *Ibid.*, p. 304.

ible transitions such as dissolves, fades, and wipes for clear punctuation.

These techniques are so common it is hard to accuse Capra of using them insidiously. What is ironic, however, is that he did employ them without question while figuring they would deliver his personal message of freedom and spontaneity. In fact his filmic system is as totalitarian and powerful as the political machinations of the film's villain, D. B. Norton. Both employ nice sentiments and the labor of the little guy to produce something unstoppable, something that can't be argued with, and, most important, something that is so monolithic that it dwarfs the pieces that gave it existence. We have learned how to analyze the monolith of the classic Hollywood system; nothing would be easier than to demonstrate the working of that discourse in *Meet John Doe*. But what gave life to this system is of the same order as that which gives life to *Meet John Doe*, a tension between the nearly military regularity and precision of the dominant discourse and the engaging lilt of the smaller voices it dares to include. The system is challenged by these small moments of counterstatement even if it ultimately harmonizes them. In *Meet John Doe* alternatives to the classic register are found first in the montage sequences prepared by Slavko Vorkapitch, and second in the individual voices of its three principal actors, speaking as they do with the trailing echo of their careers, bringing to the spectator an intimacy won in other films, in radio interviews, in magazine stories, and other organs of publicity. As Capra wanted to speak his own mind even within the world of Hollywood, so Vorkapitch, Cooper, Stanwyck, and Brennan seem to want to speak their own way within the prison of the film's logic.

THE montage sequence is one of the few clear legacies of the silent film carried over into the 1930s. It remains almost indigestible in the belly of the classic Hollywood system, for although functioning to benefit that system, it disobeys the rules we have constructed to describe that system, rules concerning invisibility of technique, clarity of development, primacy of character, and most crucially, homogeneity of narration.

By the time of *Meet John Doe*, of course, the etiquette of such sequences had been firmly conventionalized: montage sequences might appear for short sections (seldom over ninety seconds) to provide narrative transitions. They had to be dispersed through the film, never threatening to take over the discourse. They were particularly appropriate as prefaces to the main body of the narrative. The conventions of their construction were just as rigorous, permitting strong juxtapositions, but no shock-cutting. Dissolves and inventive wipes must ease the viewer through the disparate visual elements. Superimpositions fading in and out sometimes result from this strategy, frequently putting a complicated graphic image atop a more stable and recognizable one, such as a word, a calendar page, the face of a key character. The sound accompaniments of montage sequences are often loosed from their narrow tracks and allowed to roam freely amongst the images. This freedom asserts itself either with a rhythmic nondiegetic score or with a concatenation of sound pieces overlayed on one another in imitation of visual dissolves.

Such wild, experimental intrafilms are justified by the syntagmatic logic of the full text so that they serve a single function, act as one syntagmatic unit. Originally they replaced titles denoting temporal, spatial, or causal change. Indeed, they might be thought of as distended dissolves between locales, the projector mysteriously winding down to show the atomic subevents and the liquid chemistry animating them which permits the movement from one scene to the next. In this way the energy of the montage segment is held in by the function it serves in the narration, a single unambiguous function; so that for all its pyrotechnics, for its seeming challenge to discursive clarity and method, the montage sequence submits to the standard logic of the Hollywood narrative voice.

All of this is precisely the case in *Meet John Doe*. The three montage sequences are equally distributed (one in the middle of each reel on the 16mm print). Their lengths are fifty-four,

fifty-seven, and thirty-two feet, that is, between a minute and
ninety seconds. They feature an average of one new image
every three seconds, but this is complicated by the use of
superimpositions, which are sometimes multiple.

The principle of contiguity behind these sequences varies
from graphic similarity, to mini-narrative, to screen direction,
to rhythmic alteration. The first such sequence is exemplary
in this regard. Gary Cooper is caught with an irate expression
on his face [5] by the press camera. That expression graces
the front page of the paper which is seen in several locales
and as an object of exchange (money and a doorbell are inserted to thematize the issue of exchange already signified by
the successive shots of the paper). Two mini-narratives find
Barbara Stanwyck madly typing (framed in a cocked low-
angle shot [4]), putting out stories that expose graft and the
scandal of medical aid to the poor. We see dirty money being
passed; we see a poor family. These little motifs are anchored
by a headline which once again asserts the priority of the
textual as the commodity of exchange. In a series of three
varied shots, papers are shown being purchased at an accelerating pace, leading to the standby of all montage sequences,
the animated graph. Here the soaring fame of John Doe as
well as the increased circulation of the paper is explicitly displayed on a grid, superimposed over mounting piles of papers.
When those papers reach a crescendo, the sequence's most
daring transformation occurs: they begin to move not upward
but forward in a march that becomes a literal march on city
hall. A caricature of the mayor fainting gives way, as it must,
to a shot of the governor trying to defend himself. The governor is given a sync-sound speech to bring us out of the
sequence, but not before a telling track in on his face match-
dissolves to the face of D. B. Norton holding binoculars and
looking back at the camera [6]. This is the introduction of
the film's last key character, and it is quite an introduction at
that.

The modes of contiguity in this sequence are many, as is
the iconography (printed words, caricatured scenes, pixillated

objects, long shots of crowds, close-ups of money, graphics). Throughout, the metaphor of circulation is explicit and with this metaphor the suggestion that every element in the sequence, and by extension in the narrative, attains its significance only in the system that moves it and that it helps move. As money passes from hand to hand, hardly mistakable is the implication that the newspaper itself is part of the system of graft it pretends to expose. We can find a similar analogy when we look to the source of the sequence's power. D. B. Norton looking back on us with his binoculars, owner of the newspaper, is the man who dictates its policies and personnel, and this includes the benign ignoramus Gary Cooper. In terms of the allegory of narration, Frank Capra finally wrests power away from Slavko Vorkapitch, the creator of the sequence, assembling the peculiar gains of the sequence into a precise and calculated summing up. Recall that the entire sequence is triggered by a trick of photography: Gary Cooper, feigning anger over a miscalled pitch, becomes a social rabble-rouser. Even the social issues he purportedly raises are only the necessary preconditions for the march of the papers and the rise of economic and political power which the sequence chronicles. It is a peculiar chronicle, suggesting in its very form the revolutionary disruption of the life of the press and the life of politics that D. B. Norton's entry into public life has caused.

The montage aesthetic, purportedly Hollywood's daring concession to experimental cinema,[4] is given full play first of all in order to make an efficient narrative gain, taking us in this instance up a chain of command from lowly Gary Cooper to the seat of political power. At the same time it thematizes the issue of free expression and spontaneous experimentation.

---

[4] Slavko Vorkapitch was revered and feared in Hollywood. An East European refugee, he had been associated with experimental projects in the twenties, most memorably in *The Life and Death of a Hollywood Extra* (1928). During the era of the classic Hollywood film he was responsible for numerous montage sequences and was regarded as a master when it came to montage. For an overview of his life and work see Vlada Petric, "The Vorkapitch Effect," *American Film*, no. 3 (March 1978).

The montage sequences are like the sudden joyous outbursts that Walter Brennan and Gary Cooper spit out on their "doohickeys [3]." This analogy permits us to theorize the aesthetics of spontaneity, or rather, extend the theorization already attempted by Adorno in the case of jazz to the aesthetics of standard cinema. The montage sequence seems exemplary in this respect, for, like the cadenza or jazz solo, it addresses us with its freedom, its authenticity, and its bravura. Yet it always is authorized by the dominant rhythm and by the rules established in the introduction of the piece, invariably returning to those rhythms and themes. Its flurry of freedom, like that of the adolescent, is played out under the eye of the parent. This is the "regressive" aspect of modern music for Adorno.[5] Similarly in the montage sequence we find the appropriation of the graphic wizardry of Vorkapitch by the ever present father, Capra, as though Capra had been holding in reserve a certain quantity of libidinal energy, not his own but borrowed, which he released at just the appropriate narrational moment. The sequence may strike us as free, but it points in only one direction. It leads us to the powerful gaze of the fascist D. B. Norton. Norton, who has been directing the action from behind the scenes all along and who now commands his motorcycle troops before dictating, with a more subtle rhetoric, the actions of Barbara Stanwyck and, hence, Cooper himself, is the story's counterpart to the storyteller Capra, whose presence we feel behind every gesture and every change of shot.

CAPRA is not a great director of actors, but he is peerless in his use of stars. The difference is instructive, and it is clearly visible in the performance of the secondary players in the film. Aside from Stanwyck, Cooper, and Brennan, the other actors are fully utilitarian. Capra chooses them for their physiognomy, leaves them on screen long enough to deliver the proper

---

[5] Theodore Adorno, "On the Fetish Character in Music and the Regression of Listening," in *The Essential Frankfort School Reader*, ed. Andrew Arato and Eike Gebhardt (New York: Urizon, 1978), pp. 270-99.

speech and gesture, then opposes this to the next functional gesture of the next mechanical character. The relative success of this method must be credited to the casting department which he dominated. More than most of his thirties triumphs, *Meet John Doe* treats its actors as cogs in a machine, cutting to them for quick reaction shots, getting their speeches across, and getting them off screen. This is so apparent because Cooper, Stanwyck, and Brennan offer a different approach, one that we are tempted to say comes from them and is opposed to Capra.

Cooper, especially, struggles to be free within his role and within the strict limits of the camera's frame and the story's time. He is boxed in for the most part [7], but certain relaxed moments find him leading the film, deflecting our interest from the intrigue, as when he mugs for Stanwyck and her photographers or recounts his lengthy and all-too-telling dream. Here Capra has given to Cooper the same sort of leash he gave Harry Langdon in the twenties, a leash jerked back when necessary. After all, Cooper's character is written as quirky, spontaneous, with an instinct for truth and for the moment. This is what makes him so attractive to Barbara Stanwyck who shares all these qualities with the addition of ambition. Stanwyck brings to her character also a quantum of authenticity which takes her nearly beyond her role. She responds to certain situations hysterically while everyone else functions smoothly even in defeat. This is evident when she throws her shoe through Connell's window in the first sequence. While she generally knows how to control this energy, indeed knows how to use it to make others pay attention, it is with a certain ultimate hysteria that she cries to Cooper in the film's last scene, fainting in his arms when her voice can say no more. Capra doubtless saw himself in her, talented and powerful within limits, authentic beyond her talent, persuading by the power of authenticity. More than Cooper, Barbara Stanwyck, especially in this role, is an emblem of the American personality, for her resourcefulness is checked by a basic sense of values which she is certain will win out in the end and which she feels, unreflectively, that she is pushing forward. Capra permits Stanwyck her hysteria because, like Vorkapitch's quasi-anarchic montage sequences, he can lock this "other" discursive register into place, can cite it, we might say, as a reference to authenticity.

Walter Brennan represents the most recalcitrant case both as character and actor. A performer of great distinction, Brennan is nonetheless in the same paradigm with Sterling Holloway and other recognizable faces/voices which the film employs conventionally. But Brennan's style is so distinct, his position in the industry so unquestioned, that he challenges every film that tries to place him securely in its narrative. No doubt this stems from the uncouth directness he exudes, whether as poor sidekick as in this and so many other films, or as deranged but honest Judge Roy Bean, for instance, a year later in William Wyler's *The Westerner*. Unlike Cooper and Stanwyck, in other words, Walter Brennan's individual power comes from the type he has always played, as though he embodies that type. Cooper and Stanwyck exist beyond their characters and are available to a limited plurality of roles, all commenting on one another.

In *Meet John Doe* the Walter Brennan type gets its fullest play. For despite his sidekick standing, Brennan actually figures the most extreme pole of the possibilities offered by the film. He is the fully unsocialized human. His response to corruption and pettiness is a return to nature, Thoreau-like in its rugged individualism, yet without thought of social benefit nor even of the values of philosophical reflection. He is treated as the natural man, peripheral to society, yet central to any consideration of what society might be [8].

In this sense we must finally find in Walter Brennan the aptest figure for Vorkapitch's discourse of montage. Both are spontaneous and playful, both are peripheral to the dominant system they nevertheless trouble and interrupt. Both operate according to some preposterous logic, with a libidinal energy threatening to the established order yet somehow necessary for that order to bring up and deal with. And just as Vorkapitch returned his gift of freedom freely to Capra, actually promoting the narration of the film, so Walter Brennan makes a gift of his own freedom in the film's conclusion, a gift to the Christ child on Christmas Eve, as he stands (still on the periphery) beside the John Doe members, cheering John on, ushering in a new holistic image of society. He too has been integrated.

IT is Walter Brennan, far more than Gary Cooper, whom the film has difficulty in socializing; the fact that Brennan's socialization arrives in the last moment, unexplained, barely noticed, and certainly not explicitly proclaimed, suggests that the film would prefer to think of him as a sidekick, going along with Gary Cooper as the Fool goes with Lear. But like Shakespeare's fools, Brennan really does refuse to be smoothed over. He is absurd in the dramatic equation, unbalanced by any ordinary scheme of character relations. An initial list of the opposing sides of characters in descending order of their commitment to the side would be:

Power and Technology (Politics)	Personal Values (Intimacy)
Hitler (implied)	Christ (implied)
D. B. Norton	Stanwyck's father
The Politicians	Stanwyck's family
Newspaper technocrats	citizens (club members)
Stanwyck	Cooper

Walter Brennan

The plot of course turns on the incongruity of Stanwyck's belonging to the world of personal values, via her father and family. By trying to appropriate Cooper at the film's outset, she hopes to put her technology at the service of intimate, nonpolitical communication. At the end, of course, it is she who must beg to be taken, as once she took; it is technology that has failed and personal communication (an embrace, a body about to hurl itself to death) that brings her forever into the arms of Cooper. But by this time, of course, Cooper has indeed become her father, as once she wanted him to be, so that in his arms she is both taken by a lover and protected by a father.

All of this makes eminent Hollywood sense, and it successfully places every character function in the film, except Walter Brennan. No one woos the "Colonel," tempting him into the social order. He exists at the end, as he did at the outset, a permanent possibility to disorder, to ultimate liberty, a possibility of the imaginary. This is graphically apparent in several of Gary Cooper's moments of decision. As the beleaguered ego, literally on stage, Cooper looks to the Colonel who stands at the exit holding $5,000 with a mischievous gleam in his eye. In front of Cooper, though, is the word of the father, which he finally pronounces in a most dutiful way.

The temptation offered by Walter Brennan places him in inverse rapport with the film's most calculating figure, the villain D. B. Norton. Both men have disdain for citizenry, a fact underlined by a dissolve from Brennan screaming to John Doe members, "Out of my way, you helots" to Norton instructing his men how to do the "cleanup operations" on the John Doe clubs. Both men act sheerly for themselves, exercising their own wills as they please. Both live in fully male societies, standing to the side and observing the everyday life they each in their own way despise. Both are, though in opposite manners, romantic figures, acting out of their own morality, or, better, their own amorality. The danger that each represents to the culture is the danger of the not-normal. It is the danger homosexuality poses to the heterosexual world, a danger seen on the one hand as attraction toward violence and fascism and on the other toward unproductive hedonism. In Capra's vocabulary Norton poses the threat from the right in strong-armed order, while the Colonel, slighter but more engaging, stands to the far left of democracy, almost to the point of anarchy.

Capra had hoped to preach a middle path, to speak with the voice of an ordinary citizen. Cooper was chosen as that citizen, placed in a battle for authority with D. B. Norton.

There in the ballpark the logic of Capra's own plot and Norton's political machine reduce Cooper to a sniveling child with one snip of the wire-cutters. Cooper, castrated, returns to the Eden of hobo life, presexual and prepolitical [8].

Capra's dream that personal values might be packaged inside a Hollywood film, like John Doe's belief for a national reawakening outside of politics, is here cut short by its own logic. Those who live by amplification and organization must die by it, particularly if they are naive enough to use it for a "good cause." This is what we learned in a strictly filmic way when the free flow of images was seen as disciplined by Vorkapitch's montage logic.

On the other side is Walter Brennan and the temptation, occasionally accepted by the major actors, to exist outside narrative desire altogether. No shot in the film has more poetic resonance than the narratively gratuitous silhouette of Cooper and Brennan playing their "doohickeys" and dancing on a freight car. This is the end of logic, the train leading to a campfire under the bridge, the smoking of a pipe, and other useless pleasures. Cooper's acting is a type of useless pleasure that Capra never fully drafted for his purposes.

It was precisely at this point (the castration of Cooper, the return to infantile life with Walter Brennan) that Capra despaired. His hundreds of pieces did indeed form that jigsaw puzzle no final scene could complete. But Capra's forthrightness here should not disarm us. A puzzle with a missing piece is not a masterpiece *manqué*; it is an incoherent work. Walter Brennan is the token of that incoherence and his gentle hold on Gary Cooper must mock every plot solution conceivable to the Hollywood mind.

It is here that the film shifts registers, leaving its public narrative tone at the ballpark and letting speak an intimate voice of conscience and a religious voice of renunciation. Vorkapitch once again is called upon but now to remake the film in sixty seconds from the point of view of Gary Cooper. Whereas Norton ruled the first montage of Cooper's rise to fame and explicitly engineered the second montage chronicling the spread of the John Doe movement across the country, this final montage neither rises nor spreads in public strength but delves, swirls like water down a sewer into the troubled psyche of Long John Willoughby as he lies catatonic beside the Colonel's campfire.

This montage is composed primarily of shots we have already seen, but reorganized troublesomely as a threat and accusation, nightmarish, until it has an effect no logic could have on Cooper. The drama turns here not on external cause-effect but on a rhythmic accumulation of evidence and longing. Without pause, Vorkapitch dissolves from Cooper retreating down a dark alleyway to a mystical view of city hall on a snowy Christmas eve.

The montage voice of Vorkapitch has here shifted functions, from the public and political to the intimate and even psychoanalytic. This prepares the way for the final shift of registers into the hieratic. Atop city hall, Christmas bells in the air, Norton stands disarmed. When Stanwyck faints into Cooper's arms, her hysteria spent, the strains of Beethoven's "Ode to Joy" fall like snow from the sky. Gary Cooper is transformed into John Doe, into Stanwyck's father, and into Jesus himself.

Banking on the aphorism "Render unto Caesar, the things that are Caesar's, and unto God the things that are God's," Capra has tried to solve the conflict of personal purity and political effectiveness both in his plot and in his situation in Hollywood as he felt Christ solved it. Or rather, he hides behind Christ when neither of them are able to solve it. The hieratic register itself is meant to hush all doubts.

Meet John Doe is one of many Hollywood films that changes its tone, its narrational strategies, and even the rules of its genre to come to an acceptable conclusion. Far from vilifying this film or its type, we should see it as exposing a tension, present in every classic Hollywood film, between an authoritative voice of traditional logic and the more spontaneous tones of actors and visible technique. Too much of our analytical energy has gone into uncovering the source of narrative

logic. From my point of view, Hollywood had always recognized the bankruptcy of the so-called classic approach, and
challenged it in every film. If the spontaneous, the playful, the
authentic subvoices in these films are put in choruses to support the same old song and singer, we ought to at least examine
the productive tension between the two.

In *Meet John Doe* this tension is palpable when the chorus
(Vorkapitch and the principal actors) is forced to finish the
song which Capra and his narrative logic have failed to end.
Stepping back from a microphone that can only whistle in
feedback, Capra lets us attend to acting as acting, technique
as technique, if only to be able to close a film he had opened.

In the classic era Hollywood always stayed on top, even in
such maverick independent productions as *Meet John Doe*.
But the adjustments that it was forced to make to drown out
or harmonize other voices, like Capra's adjustments in *Meet
John Doe*, are ingenious and fertile. Hollywood is most interesting when its authoritative voice is in question. It is in
question, I believe, a good part of the time. For spectators
and analysts alike, the complications this struggle for unifi-
cation produces ought to be of far more interest than the
sameness of the system we have so prematurely labeled "classic."

CHAPTER SIX

La Symphonie pastorale
Performed by the French
Quality Orchestra

IF literature has often come to the aid of cinema, it has never done so more dramatically than in postwar France. From 1945 to 1948 that country was beset with ugly internal strife (including industrial *épuration*, the barring of personnel on the basis of the merest suspicion of relations with the occupying regime), beleaguered from without by the invasion of 1,800 American films beginning to pour onto the Continent, and constrained by economic and production woes that made financing a film difficult and creation of a finished product uncertain.

The French response, proclaimed in the very first issue of the official *Le Cinéma Français* in 1945, was contained in a single word, "quality." France's literary past was invoked as both a model and a source for the "quality" films that would dominate the industry until well into the fifties.

A fully ideological term, "quality" was opposed to Hollywood's "quantitative" industry based on a huge number of films and immense budgets for certain pictures. Without these resources, the French system, it was felt, could survive only by exploiting the good taste, intelligence, and ingenuity of its personnel, attributes fostered by a production mechanism modeled not like Hollywood on the assembly line but on the image of an "équipe" of artists and artisans working in a

This chapter was first published, in a slightly different form, in *Modern European Filmmakers and the Art of Adaption*, edited by Andrew S. Horton and Joan Magretta (New York: Ungar, 1981).

revered tradition on a revered project. No project was more suited to this conception of film art than adaptation, for here the project was by definition honorable and the market already prepared. Dependent for solvency on foreign distribution, it was only good business for the French to draw on their internationally renowned literary past. Perhaps more important, the values, both aesthetic and moral, of that literary past promised to grant an economically weak cinema some veneer of maturity.

The maturity and good taste of the cinema of quality was fabled even to the point of complacency and self-satisfaction. Graphically these films looked like perfectly dressed store windows. Narratively they were tidy, an abstract moral problem translated into a perfect dramatic equation solved without remainder. Theatrically trained actors, sporting costumes by Christian Dior and other tasteful but trend-setting *couturiers*, delivered pithy and formal dialogue in voices meant not for the other characters in the drama but for an audience paying to see spectacle, performance, and culture—in short, paying to see quality.

The stodgy studio look of these films, their conservative editing styles, and their cold impersonal atmosphere turned the world's opinion against them, following Truffaut's devastating attack of 1954, "A Certain Tendency in French Cinema."[1] If this era still calls to us at all, it is mainly because of its relation to literature, for while we today may decry public and showcase cinema in favor of personal and spontaneous works, nevertheless most of us are ready to acknowledge that the treasure chest of literary classics might demand a different sort of treatment. Privileged to live in the present as remnants of the past, great novels seem to call for reverential treatment, for vellum bindings and quality adaptations. Of such adaptations few seem worthier than Jean Delannoy's version of

---

[1] François Truffaut, "A Certain Tendency in French Cinema," in *Movies and Methods*, ed. Bill Nichols (Berkeley and Los Angeles: University of California Press, 1976), pp. 224-36. The original essay appeared in *Cahiers du Cinéma*, No. 31 (January 1954).

Gide's *La Symphonie pastorale*, a film that took first place at Cannes in 1946.

Jean Delannoy was born to direct this film. Protestant and circumspect, he has always been considered a "cold" director obsessed by moral and metaphysical questions, yet one who invariably found success at the box office. His first films date from 1938 and showed immediately a facility in many genres. Yet it was only with *L'Eternal Retour* (1943), which he directed under the close collaboration of Jean Cocteau as scenarist, that Delannoy's style and preoccupations became clear.

La Symphonie pastorale suited his temperament perfectly and, because of its literary fame and the renown of the cast, was the subject of tremendous publicity. The critical and popular success enjoyed by this film secured Delannoy an unshakeable position in the French film industry and tempted him to risk other abstract subjects. He immediately directed Jean-Paul Sartre's first original script, *Les Jeux sont faits* (1947) and later, his other masterpiece, *Dieu a besoin des hommes* (1949), from the celebrated novel by Henri Queffelec.

Critical opinion began to turn against him in the fifties because of the predictability of his treatments and the lifelessness of the acting in his films. By the time Truffaut excoriated him in 1954 he was at best considered a reliable studio director, cranking out too many films a year, the most ambitious of which were historical or literary spectaculars. After 1950 little new was expected of Delannoy, but in 1945 the whole film community of France anticipated a work of genius or at least of exactness and propriety, presumably the qualities perfectly suited to the adaptation of a work by André Gide.

To watch *La Symphonie pastorale* today, then, is to perform a complex interpretive task. On the one hand we can only be impressed by the rigid precision and carefulness of the film's production values. It is a beautiful film to look at and yet apparently self-restrained. For example, we shall see that its mountain scenery forms a structural, not decorative value. *La Symphonie pastorale* lets us appreciate a kind of film, which, due to its pomposity, we have difficulty today in listening to. The name André Gide doubtless forces our attention and indulgence.

But it is this same André Gide who will, I think, ultimately make us share Truffaut's unfavorable judgment of this film. While the overall style of the cinema of quality may render the tone of the novella with uncanny purity, the rigidity of that style was inadequate to the subtleties Gide built into his discourse, particularly in relation to point of view. And so we have a wonderful example of a type of film worth looking at, but a type that, though especially dependent on adaptation, was not supple enough to do justice to the literature it celebrated. Film historians may find themselves wholly satisfied, while literary scholars may be profoundly disappointed, as, in fact, was Gide himself. All will agree, however, that if *La Symphonie pastorale* were ever to be adapted, this was the epoch in film history prepared and eager for the task. Gide saw this clearly.

In having created a novella that is at once lean and richly coded with traditional imagery, he knew he couldn't have obliged Delannoy further. The intricacies of the plot form a moral equation, which the French cinema had learned how to present and solve. The brevity of the original (some seventy pages) reduced immediately the inevitable complaints about editing and expurgation. Finally, Gide's classical style and the elegant structure of the book were eminently suited to the cultural voice of quality cinema, a voice at once elevated and correct.

The moral equation is not the least of Gide's achievements in this work. A Calvinist pastor, happening upon a wretched blind abandoned child, devotes his energy and life to her bettering, bringing her into the light of the intellect even while he neglects his own wife and children. The Christian love in which he instructs her is complicated by the erotic love he obviously feels for her and only partially represses. The crisis comes at the moment of her cure, when, seeing life to be discordant and murky, she throws herself suicidally into the river, leaving the pastor alone, his family disconsolate and dispersed.

The exquisite mixture of anti-clerical and erotic material in Gide's *La Symphonie pastorale* (1918) was perfectly suited to the temperament and ideology of postwar French culture, particularly the subculture in control of the film industry. As Truffaut was to point out, the "liberal" sentiments of this group were self-righteous in the extreme. Toying with the blasphemous as well as with the titillating, cinema of quality preached in film after film a progressivist, even Freemason attitude toward life.

As a matter of fact, the adaptation shies away from the theological subdrama of the novella (including Gertrude's conversion to Catholicism) and presents the pastor's relation to Gertrude as more chaste than had Gide. But this is only one more indication of the sort of decorum sought after in this era, a decorum rent apart a decade later by such sexually explicit films as Vadim's *And God Created Woman* (1956) and Malle's *The Lovers* (1958). It was enough in 1946 to suggest the erotic and to ridicule the seriousness of religion without treating either of these subjects in a thorough fashion.

Instead, the interest of the adaptation buys into the dramatic rendering of these themes via a symmetrical development of characters. While the novella continually stretches back in time to give weight to its action and while it modulates all action through the eyes and thoughts of the pastor, the film spreads out our interest across an entire field of characters. Indeed, a new character, Piette, is invented for this very purpose, embodying a choice for the pastor's son, Jacques, analogous to the role the pastor's family plays for him. As the pastor rejects his family in favor of Gertrude so does Jacques relinquish Piette for her. The film takes note of the consequences of these decisions by inserting several key reaction shots and even a couple of point-of-view shots of the betrayed parties. In all fairness it must be noted that in his original adaptation of the novella (spurned by Delannoy),

Gide too had added a female character for Jacques, but she played a lesser role.

The balancing of the dramatic equation has its counterpart in the regularizing of the dramatic rhythm of the original. It was this aspect that frustrated Gide and ostensibly caused his break with Delannoy. The novella, Gide claims,

> Makes sense only in terms of its artistic construction. It is, in sum, a tragedy in five acts which takes on its final value only through the long night of the first four acts. The young blind girl recovers her sight only in the last pages—to her detriment as it turns out. Everything resides in this sudden rupture. They explained to me that the necessities of the screen warranted a new conception of the tale, that it had to be translated into another language.[2]

Delannoy gives Gertrude her sight some two-thirds of the way through the film. This is, as Gide notes, entirely consistent with dominant film narrative practice, but it has the effect of softening and stabilizing that which originally was frighteningly abrupt. But Delannoy worked within his rights here, for, having taken the tale out of the hands of the pastor and spread it among a whole field of characters, the decisive reversal of Gertrude's blindness needs to affect everyone in turn. Gide's original delivers the experience of such a reversal through the mind of the drama's most passionate character, and the brutally swift conclusion is consonant with the overall ironic effect, which has repeatedly overturned the pastor's thoughts and desires throughout at least the entire second half of the novella.

Delannoy's decision to incorporate Gide's irony entirely within the plot rather than in the telling of the tale was, I'm certain, quite unconscious. It was sheer instinct, the unques-

[2] André Gide in *Ecran Français*, No. 65, September 25, 1946. Gide's script and some discussion of the circumstances under which it was written appear in André Gide, *La Symphonie pastorale*, ed. Claude Martin (Paris: Minard, 1970).

tioned work of a certain conception of film. On the one hand, French cinema at this time was hardly capable of subtle narrational strategies. On the other, an invisible pressure assured the presentation of a clean and balanced picture of events: every tale and every style was turned into that "other language" Gide spoke of, the language of cinema of quality.

In practice, aside from deletions, additions, and dramatic restructuring, what does this mean? Primarily it concerns the construction of a totally satisfying picture of dramatic tensions and releases, a picture that, either in one shot or built up through a relation of a few adjacent shots, symmetrically holds the film's values in place. For example, a single powerful shot culminates the tension within and between father and son in their attempt to possess the unseeing Gertrude, a tension ascribed to the possessiveness of sight itself. Vision distances them from each other and from her. In her world of touch (the shots of hands) and sound, she alone can be happy. Delannoy sums up this situation at the end of a quarrel between father and son, when both characters walk to a window and gaze out from the dark foreground at Gertrude sitting in the garden [2]. This shot is the apotheosis of the first half of the drama, and it gains in appeal by mimicking the spectator's own situation, looking through a glass toward an object one can see but an object that can't return the gaze, the luminous film itself and the blind sexuality at its heart.

The next act of the drama is inaugurated by the operation that restores Gertrude's sight. Her emergence from the hospital after the cure is given to us in three shots: her light cape and dark hair set her off against the two dark-clad nuns with white veils who support each of her arms in a frontal midshot; she frees herself from them, and, as she breathes in her first vision of the world, a cut to an extreme long shot liberates her in a thrilling way yet contains her [6]. The liberation results from the distance of the shot, expressing the sudden expansion of her horizons; it comes as well from the puffy flakes of studio snow which both bless her cure from heaven and recall the snowy origins out of which she was snatched.

But simultaneously she is caught in a perfectly composed shot, which serves almost to enclose her in a glass ball paperweight. The church behind her, the signs of nature before her, and the dark nuns on her sides lock her in a pleasing position. She is radiant at the center of this configuration, yet she is trapped within its artificial structure. Delannoy can then move in for a final big close-up of her face, amazed at the spectacle of life before her. Her pleasure in seeing compounds our pleasure. Her gratitude to God is simultaneously our gratitude to this film. For a moment the world and the film are glorious visual symphonies, harmonious arrangements of physical and moral properties.

When the dramatic tension resides not within a single character but is suspended between two or more characters, compositions and lighting are opposed in almost comic book fashion. Arriving at the church, Gertrude finds her way to Amelie's side, all eyes looking at her eyes. Amelie signals to her that the man in the pulpit is the pastor and we are then given, predictably enough, an exchange of glances between her and the pastor which derives its impact in large part from the fact that *she* can now actually glance at *him*. From her point of view he looms above the congregation, almost ready to pitch foward from his perch. He is dark and severe, a bit ridiculous in his assumed authority. The reverse angle encloses Gertrude in a web of compositional lines formed by the other members of the congregation. Her light cape is highlighted by a key light. In this sea of forms before the pastor she stands out as an object-choice. A second reprise of this pair of shots is dramatized when the pastor breaks the stunned silence of the moment by invoking a prayer of thanksgiving, spreading his arms as he does so. This threatrical gesture carries connotations of crucifixion from Gertrude's point of view, but in cutting behind him for the reverse angle, we see him suddenly as a bird of prey ready to swoop down on Gertrude, who is caught in the center of the frame and nearly blotted out by his backlit figure in the foreground.

This hieratic style retains vestiges of realism even while it continually shapes its reality into tableaux and set pieces. Indeed, the formality of the adaptation can be seen to accord with the literary source being treated. Gestures and views are meticulously constructed in the manner of a literary scene. The frozen effects of cinema of quality seem justified, in general, by the past tense within which all literary works can be said to exist, and in particular by the journal structure of this novella, a structure that carefully dates each entry. The style of the film, then, is appropriately a memorializing one. Even its slight attempts at dramatic camerawork, such as the cocked angles and the frequent track-ins on faces, have an academic feel which vitiates any immediacy they might otherwise have attained [4]. In Clouzot's *Le Corbeau* (1943) or even in Carol Reed's *Odd Man Out* (1947) such angles and camera movements strive to involve the viewer corporally in the drama. But Delannoy insists on structure over experience, solidifying dramatic tensions through camerawork which we are asked to note and appreciate but which doesn't demand our participation [3, 5]. There is a glass between the viewer and this film, the glass of the store window barring us from the action and asking us to hold it visually in place, to understand it, but certainly not to enter it or to help construct it ourselves. The cinema of quality descends to the viewer from on high, from some seat of visual taste and elegance which graces the movie theater, and from a memorable literary past which is beyond normal experience even as it treats of such experience.

The haughty coolness of Delannoy's personal brand of quality direction has made him scorned by progressive film critics, but it did allow him to achieve some remarkable effects in *La Symphonie pastorale*, effects that placed it among those postwar adaptations singled out by André Bazin as daring and innovative.[3] For Bazin, Delannoy discovered in the omnipresent snow of his decor [7] a visual equivalent for Gide's simple preterate sentences. Both are clear and chilling. Both set off

---

[3] André Bazin, *What Is Cinema?* trans. Hugh Gray (Berkeley and Los Angeles: University of California Press, 1967), pp. 66-68.

the moral drama crisply. Both connote fatality and a certain spiritual dryness, an emotion (or lack of it) with which Gide, employing an ironic geographical reversal in his imagery, closes his tale: "I wanted to pray but I felt my heart to be as arid as a desert."

Bazin's disciple, Amédée Ayfre, writing years later, was even more exuberant about the snow.

There is a secret correspondence between physical and moral blindness so that this snow, which blocks vision and softens the edges of forms, reduces all oppositions and fills in crevices returning the world to its state of primeval cloudiness beyond good and evil. Thanks to the silent consonance between a human visage and a snowy landscape, there is thus instantiated the creation of certain values which cast the metamorphosis of Fate across this tragedy of passion and feeling.[4]

The snow is part of the crude symbolism with which the pastor organizes his experience, and this the filmmakers were quick to make use of. The dualism of the sense of touch, Gertrude's primary way of knowing the world yet the seat of sensual and sexual engagement, is exploited through continual close-ups of hands. The clarity that distinguishes sight among all the senses is shown to be an alienating knife, not only through the calculated looks the characters give one another and the more calculating look of the camera that isolates characters, but by the placid non-look of Michele Morgan as Gertrude. To insist on this effect Delannoy has recourse to frequent shots of characters before mirrors, Gertrude "looking past" this other sort of window, the pastor arrested by the sight of himself and his protegé. Gertrude senses light by feeling the heat pouring through the windows. She has a tactile relation to vision that vitalizes her and paradoxically unites her with the world.

---

[4] Amédée Ayfre in Henri Agel and A. Ayfre, *Le Cinéma et le sacre* (Paris: Editions de Cerf, 1961), p. 169.

Delannoy's determination to insist on these paradoxes and symbols only amplified his native instinct for the handling of actors, an instinct that does not wear well and that was abhorred even in its own day.[5] Aside from Michele Morgan, who is quite literally a blind vision and who is photographed in her natural beauty, the other actors present their characters to us in melodramatic fashion. One can almost see them thinking through their spiritual state before locating the precise tone or gesture to carry that state to us [1]. The parts are conned in advance, carefully weighed and heavily expressed. Delannoy exaggerates this pretentious seriousness by reducing the indoor decor to a minimum in most scenes, by toning down the lighting to an effective modulation of the middle grey scale [3], and by playing the dialogue to the audience through cutting to front shots when the actors stray too far from their 45-degree, open shoulder deliveries. Cocked angles and expressionist shadowing punctuate the truly "significant" scenes as visual exclamation marks [4].

The extent to which abstract character interrelations dominate this film is made apparent whenever a highly concrete object or image appears. The pastor clinking the steaming bowl of broth with the spoon while calling "Petite, petite, petite," and the Bach prelude that Jacques plays are good examples. They suggest as well the slight attention given by Delannoy to the sound track, a strange inattention, especially in view of the film's title and of the overt opposition Gide created between aural harmony and visual heterogeneity. True, Gertrude becomes the church's organist, but we don't experience her world of sound. She exists entirely within a web of speeches and ideas. Her blind sensuality, present as an unconscious horizon in Gide's novella, is tamed by Delannoy until we feel that she knows everything about the world except its visible properties, properties that surprise her but that don't alter her fundamental relation to life. In Gide, of course, the

---

[5] Pierre Leprohon, *Présences Contemporaines (Cinéma)* (Paris: Editions Debresses, 1956), pp. 312-13, 318.

impossibility of correlating sight and sound becomes a key analogy in suggesting the impossibility of correlating the world of experience and that of morality.[6] Furthermore, Gide's pastor senses Gertrude as an altogether primitive and foreign quantity which erupts in his life and causes him to pit Jesus against St. Paul. Delannoy more discreetly and weakly suggests that the pastor must choose between two women, one attractive and the other one to whom he owes a duty. Gertrude's blindness becomes in the film merely the dramatic precondition of a conventional temptation.

The conventionality of the film is increased by the background music of Georges Auric, which exchanges one of Gide's key elements (the Beethoven) for ordinary film music. The dictates of "the normal large film-going public"[7] were also responsible for the introduction of Mr. Castelan, a wealthy burgher, and his carefully appointed bourgeois home. It was as if the filmmakers became afraid that audiences would clamor for their money back if they didn't get a glimpse of well-lit living rooms with lots of crystal. Castalan further obliges the popular taste by playing a broadly comic role. Far from setting off the austere presbytery and its morally wracked inhabitants, Castelan and his daughter, Piette, spread out the dramatic forces of the plot and allow the spectator to enter it from wherever it seems comfortable.

Here we encounter the most serious breach in adaptation, for Gide's novella attains its interest by refusing to allow the reader a comfortable entry into the tale. We are rigorously restricted to the tortured conscience and consciousness of the pastor. While he is self-deceived, his own gradual awareness of that self-deception redeems him before us or, in any case, does not allow us easily to judge him. The notorious Gidean irony was never more far-reaching and complex than here. By making the pastor merely another character (even though

[6] Zachary T. Ralston, "Synesthesia in Gide's *La Symphonie pastorale*," The Citadel Monograph Series, no. 15 (Charleston, S.C., 1976).

[7] Pierre Bost, quoted in Henri Jeanson, *Soixante-dix ans d'adolescence* (Paris: Stock, 1976).

the most important character), the filmmakers have displayed a story in front of us objectively, and given us the means to judge. The pastor is guilty! The film is a mere exposé of hypocrisy and the "normal" characters of Piette and Castelan are shown to be duped by a sanctimonious cleric. In Gide there are no "normal characters" and certainly no normal perspectives.

In contrast to the novella, the storytelling of this film knows no bounds and is tied to no principle save expediency and clarity. Its feeble effort to replicate the pastor's hindsight occurs through the cascade of "cahiers" which dissolve into one another and mark the growth of the little blind girl into Michele Morgan. But at the same time the camera feels free to elaborate scenes at which the pastor is absent (most notably the silent meeting of Jacques and Gertrude at the hospital [3, 5]) and generally to observe the reactions of all characters. The effect of the knot of the plot is thus generalized among the characters and laid out in all its simplicity before the audience.

Surely this did have the effect of popularizing Gide's novella, but at the expense of its real interest, the interplay between action and reflection. The symbols of snow, symphony, mirrors, hands, of light and dark, and so forth are potent but naive. Gide, who could never present them in his own name, takes pleasure in allowing the pastor to consider life through them. The inadequacy of such symbolization is the major irony of the tale. And yet, by taking the tale out of the pastor's hands, the filmmakers perpetuate the very simple-minded symbolism the novella questions. Thus, through its self-righteous style, a style insisting on total narrative command and the urbane presentation of its material, the cinema of quality has fallen dupe to a novella that almost seemed too simple for it but that escaped it by means of the calculated limitation of its presentation. In a very real sense the filmmakers, who have confidently gone beyond and judged the moral blindness of the pastor, are unequal to the complications of his style. Their own eminently public style showcases the situation but cannot reflect upon it. Gide's book has been put forever in a store window through this adaptation, but it has not thereby been read by those who gaze at it. A coffee-table vellum version, Delannoy's adaptation was most valuable for sending some of its millions of viewers back to the pastor's untidy cahiers, back that is, to read Gide.

CHAPTER SEVEN

Private Scribblings: The Crux in the Margins around *Diary of a Country Priest*

LITERARY adaptation was the saving grace of the French postwar quality tradition and its most ample source of inspiration, but it was also, along with the short film, the means and locus of challenge to this tradition. The ethos, the very value of French cinema, was never more directly questioned than in Robert Bresson's 1951 *Diary of a Country Priest*, a film that, because of its austere and spiritual subject matter as well as its "diary" format, one cannot help comparing to *La Symphonie pastorale*.

"After Bresson, Aurenche and Bost are but the Viollet-le-Duc of cinematographic adaptation."[1] With this lethal sentence, indicting the scenarists of *La Symphonie pastorale* and the architects of the cinema of quality by reference to one of the most notorious architectural "restorers" in history, Bazin concludes his essay "*Le Journal d'un curé de campagne* and the Stylistics of Robert Bresson," an essay called by its translator, without hyperbole, the "most perfectly wrought piece of film criticism" ever written.[2]

This image of Jean Aurenche and Pierre Bost as the prettifiers and popularizers of literary classics was to be taken up, with infinitely more malice, by Bazin's young protegé François Truffaut in his first major essay, "A Certain Tendency in

---

This chapter was first published, in a slightly different form, in *Modern European Filmmakers and the Art of Adaption*, edited by Andrew S. Horton and Joan Magretta (New York: Ungar, 1981).

[1] André Bazin, *What is Cinema?* trans. Hugh Gray (Berkeley and Los Angeles: University of California Press, 1967), p. 143.

[2] *Ibid.*, translator's "Introduction," p. 7.

French Cinema."[3] Once again *Diary of a Country Priest* becomes the *cause célèbre*, the literary masterpiece wrested from the overweening hands of these "professionals" and given over to a true man of the cinema, Robert Bresson. With delectation, Truffaut recounts the humiliating reception Aurenche and Bost's script was given by the novel's author shortly before his death in 1948 and the joy thereafter in the world of letters as well as the world of cinema when Robert Bresson's version was accepted enthusiastically.

What had Aurenche and Bost done? They had done what they always did! They had cinematized a trenchantly literary work by balancing characters and tightening dialogue into pithy maxims; they had dramatized small scenes with flamboyant acts and gestures. Specifically, Truffaut notes, they had eliminated Dr. Delbende because (so Aurenche claimed) "Perhaps in ten years a scenarist will be able to retain a character who dies midway in the film, but as for me I find myself simply unable to do that."[4] They had rearranged key speeches, going so far as to conclude the film with a minor character's despairing cry, "When you're dead everything is dead," instead of Bernanos's "What does it matter, all is grace." And, in their most excessive act of "clarification," they had turned Bernanos's delicate dialogue between Chantal and the curé in the confessional into a scene both farcical and blasphemous, in which the girl spits out a consecrated host. This was especially outrageous because Bresson, in his version, would follow precisely the cues in the novel ("her face began to appear little by little, by degrees" [1, 2]),[5] not only expressing the incident with classic purity but also painting one of the most haunting scenes in the history of the cinema.

---

[3] François Truffaut, "A Certain Tendency in French Cinema," in *Movies and Methods*, ed. Bill Nichols (Berkeley and Los Angeles: University of California Press, 1976), pp. 224-37. The original appeared in *Cahiers du Cinéma*, No. 31 (January 1954).

[4] Cited by Truffaut, *ibid.*, p. 236.

[5] Georges Bernanos, *The Diary of a Country Priest*, trans. Pamela Morris (Toronto: Macmillan, 1937), p. 118.

Truffaut's indiscretion in publicizing this sordid failure by the pillars of French cinema did not go unnoticed. He was, as is well known, ostracized from the French film community and forced to build his reputation upon spite and disgruntlement. Even today much of that community has not forgiven him. The scriptwriter Henri Jeanson grows livid recalling the incident, detailing how Truffaut sweet-talked Bost out of a copy of the rejected script by telling him he adored his work, only to scribble down every scene or line with which he might later embarrass Bost.[6] But actually Truffaut adds nothing new to the store of examples detailed by Bernanos himself in a 1948 article about the problems with the adaptation.[7] Bernanos was displeased not only with the Aurenche-Bost submission but also with Aurenche's published account of his difficulties negotiating with the famous author. Nevertheless, while excoriating the liberties taken with his novel, Bernanos encouraged other scenarists to try their hand at "dreaming his novel over again in the language of the cinema," for he had been genuinely excited by the idea of the adaptation, especially since Jean-Louis Barrault wanted the lead role desperately, and Bernanos had loved him in *Children of Paradise*.[8]

Bernanos was not unfamiliar with scriptwriting. Indeed, at that very time he was composing his last work, a screenplay called *Dialogue of the Carmelites*. His close friend Raymond Bruckberger, a Dominican priest, was putting this production together with the noted cameraman Philippe Agostini. Bruckberger had previous experience as a producer and had, in fact, been responsible for Bresson's first feature, *Les Anges du péché* (1943). Agostini had photographed that film as well as *Les Dames du Bois du Boulogne*. Even with this experience, and even with the best wishes of Bernanos, their efforts this time

[6] Henri Jeanson, *Soixante-dix ans d'adolescence* (Paris: Stock, 1975), p. 442.

[7] Bernanos, in *Samedi-Soir*, November 8, 1947.

[8] Robert Speaight, *Georges Bernanos* (London: Collins and Harville, 1973), p. 261.

1

2

3

4

Evil Eye also watches.

5

6

7

8

1

2

3

4

5

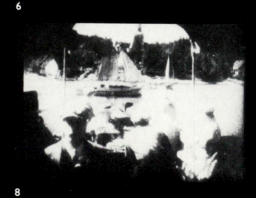

6

7

8

9

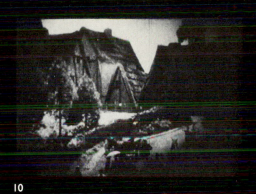

10

11

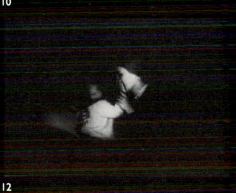

12

13

14

15

16

17

18

19

20

21

"Couldn't she get drowned?"

22

23

24

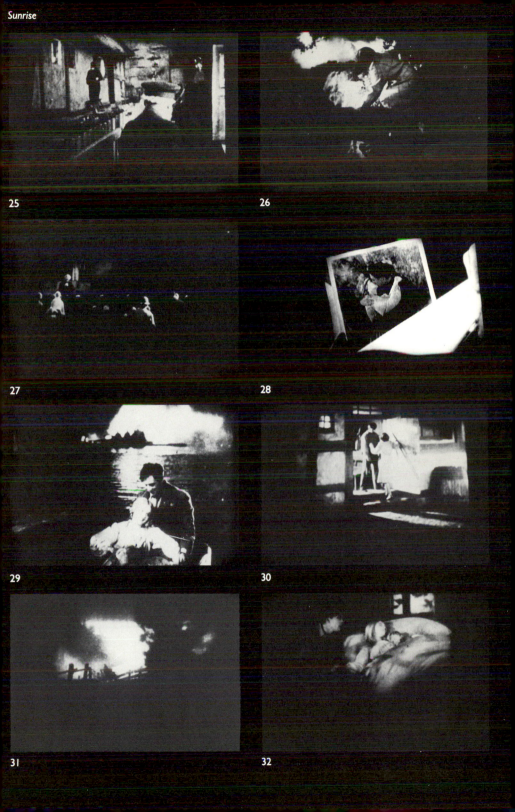

25

26

27

28

29

30

31

32

2

3   4

5   6

7   8

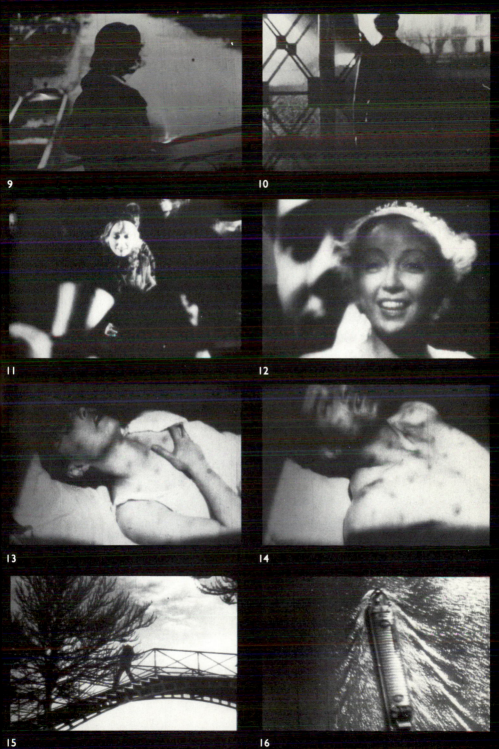

9

10

11

12

13

14

15

16

1

2

3

4

5

6

7

8

Symphonie pastorale

She is loved . . . she's happy . . .

Henry V

1

2

3

4

5

6

7

8

1

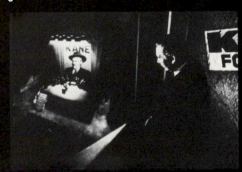

2

3

4

5

6

7

8

9

10

11

12

13

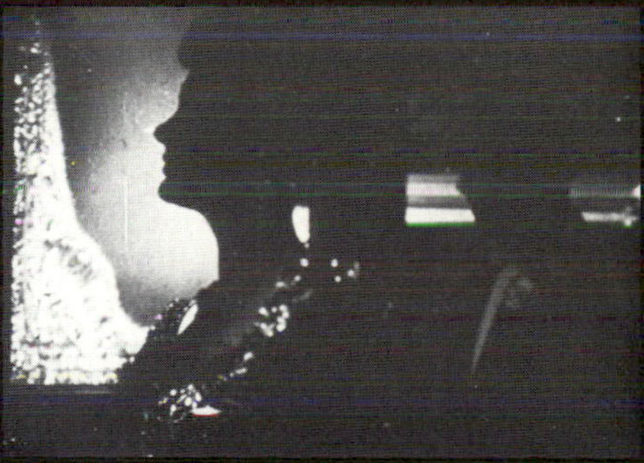

14

15

16

17

18

19

20

21

22

23

24

Kenji Mizoguchi

1

2

3

4

5

6

7

8

Kenji Mizoguchi

9

10

11

12

13

14

15

16

"Our love was wrong..."

failed, and the shooting was canceled. Later, of course, Albert Béguin resuscitated *Dialogue of the Carmelites* and produced it for the stage with great success. It became the basis for Francis Poulenc's 1956 operatic masterpiece and was finally brought to the screen in 1960 by Bruckberger and Agostini, although with a great many alterations and little subsequent praise.

It was only natural for Bruckberger in 1948 to take up Bernanos's challenge regarding *Diary* while they were working on *Dialogue of the Carmelites*. Bruckberger could not keep himself from rewriting the novel in the atmosphere of the Occupation, for he had been the chief chaplain of the Maquis, entering Paris at de Gaulle's elbow. While the tone of sordid collaboration in the parish which he invented doubtless clarified and tightened the curé's anxiety, this moral specificity couldn't have been more false to the "general" condition of spiritual loneliness which Bernanos had so forcefully created in 1934 by setting the curé's tribulations in the pastoral indifference of a quiet village. This modernization was unacceptable to Bernanos.

It was also in 1948 that Bresson began to compose his version at the behest of an ambitious young producer, Pierre Gerin. With Bernanos's death in July 1948, however, and after a perusal of Bresson's austere and unconventional script, Gerin pulled out and sold his rights to Bresson. When Bernanos's literary executor, Albert Béguin, editor of *Esprit*, accepted Bresson's proposal, the French national production agency, Union Général du Cinéma, agreed to back the film as a special one-time venture.

The story of the making of the film has been recounted often.[9] Bresson chose for his hero a young Swiss actor from among a great many candidates, all practicing Catholics. For over a year Bresson and Claude Laydu met each Sunday to

[9] See especially Pierre Leprohon, *Présences Contemporaines (Cinéma)* (Paris: Editions Debresse, 1957), pp. 363-65; and Michel Esteve, "Bernanos et Bresson," *Archives Bernanos*, No. 7 (1978), 39-52.

discuss the role. Laydu lived for a time in a monastery to accustom himself to priestly gestures so that he would, in Bresson's formulation, no longer be an actor but a model, a pure form, unconscious and instinctive, to be sculpted by light and camera.

Most of the other actors were nonprofessionals, usually acquaintances with whose faces Bresson felt familiar. The shooting, which lasted from March to May 1950, took place in the precise area of Bernanos's ancestral home, the north coast of Calais. Plagued with uncharacteristically sunny weather, Bresson worked endlessly on the minutiae of the indoor sequences, all of which were shot in the buildings of the area.

The French press covered the making and premiere of the film with awe and pride.[10] They helped guide it to a new audience consisting of intellectuals and the pious—people who seldom went to the cinema. They also encouraged cinephiles to see this particular film more than once. In this way *Diary of a Country Priest* opened up new options in the conception, realization, and exploitation of a film.

By insisting on his rigorous conception and by refusing the slightest compromise, Bresson knew he was flying in the face of the tradition of quality and specifically its premier scenarists, Aurenche and Bost. He felt justified, and the French press justified him on the basis of the precious subject which he had chosen and which in a way had chosen him. It was, in other words, the special status of adaptation that allowed this break in standard film practice. In a sense, because of Bernanos, Bresson was given license to attack everything *La Symphonie pastorale* stood for, and he implicitly recognized the politics of the situation. Later, in 1953, he uncharacteristically brought this struggle into the open by exchanging a series of semi-public letters with Jean Delannoy over the rights to Mme. de La Fayette's *La Princesse de Cleves*, certain that the punctilious Delannoy would deaden this treasured classic and personal favorite, as he had Gide's novella. Bresson lost

---

[10] See, for instance, *Unifrance*, May 1950 and September 1951.

the dispute, and Delannoy eventually made a predictably forgettable film, predictable because, as his scenarist Pierre Bost admitted: "After all, authors live with their novels for a lifetime, while we are with them only for a moment."[11] Bresson, who could never accept such lack of ambition, found this attitude consummately unacceptable in regard to adaptation; he wanted to serve literature by allowing it to compel a cinematic style worthy of the original. *Diary of a Country Priest* is perhaps the first adaptation fully forged under such a compulsion.

Although the adaptation of an important literary work provided Bresson with the occasion to challenge the aesthetics of the French filmmaking industry, his challenge in fact involved far more than the single issue of fidelity. Essentially, Bresson's film overturns the notions of the "cinematic story" and the "primacy of the image." Whereas French quality cinema is architectural, theatrical, public, clear, gaudy, and conventional, Bresson's *Diary of a Country Priest* is, on the contrary, fluid, musical, interior, obscure, ascetic, and idiosyncratic.

Nor can these differences be attributed entirely to the genre within which Bresson was working—the spiritual film—although undoubtedly the film industry could applaud his work while dismissing its challenge by cataloguing it in that way. In fact, as we have seen, *La Symphonie pastorale* would have to be classified together with *Diary*, and with numerous other postwar French films. No, Bresson's *Diary* goes to the heart of the question "What is cinema?" by implying that the French quality system, including all its varieties and subjects, forms but one overworked genre itself, morally and aesthetically innocuous but pragmatically lethal in its power to choke out other options.

Bresson had always exhibited the self-righteous strength which energized this vaster conception of cinema. His first two features, both shot during the Occupation, were considered rigorous and demanding, even though they utilized qual-

---

[11] Bost, quoted in Jeanson, p. 422.

ity actors, decorators, and technical personnel and even though they epitomized the studio approach to filmmaking. In these early days he seemed to be an aberration within the system, one whom the system could readily handle and from whom it could reap a measure of prestige among artists and intellectuals.

But *Diary of a Country Priest* marks a nearly total rejection of the old, and the birth of a new, system. One can see this from the published *Notes on Cinematography*, the first entries of which date from 1950. This new system would be based, Bresson claims, not on a notion of the construction of a film but on *écriture*, on cinematic writing. The potency of this term cannot be underestimated. It is a term that gained some measure of common usage after the war and was, perhaps unconsciously, thrown up against "quality." Alexandre Astruc's famed 1948 essay "Le Caméra stylo" fully polemicized the concept, handing it over to filmmakers like Bresson and Resnais and giving them a recognizable alternative to the dominant theatrical film.[12]

Écriture carried with it a special notion of *auteur*, a notion different from the legal denotation of "those responsible for the realization of the film." For Astruc, for Bresson, and a bit later for Truffaut, an *auteur* was a man of the cinema engaged in forging a personal style adequately responsive to the situation as the artist in history. This Sartrean terminology came via Astruc's reverence for and friendship with the famous thinker whose articles were shaping a whole generation's vocabulary as they appeared month after month in *Les Temps Modernes*. Sartre's crucial essay "What is Literature?" is dated 1947.

Bresson, being neither a man of letters nor an intellectual, took up the vocabulary of Astruc, and through him of Sartre, only because it provided him with the critical resources he needed in his internal battle with the film culture of the day.

[12] Alexandre Astruc, "Le Caméra stylo," in *The New Wave*, ed. Peter Graham (Garden City, N.Y.: Doubleday, 1968), pp. 17-24.

The vast majority of Bresson's published notes are negative in tone as he warns himself over and over against falling to the temptations of theatricality, solidification, and compromise. But his notes insist on positive programs as well, on ways of working that could release new powers from himself and the world by activating the atrophied limbs of cinema.

Bresson is concerned to rethink completely the notions of the actor, the shot, and the sound track. More important is his strategy of total discipline and control put at the service of discovery, that is, at the service of the spontaneous revelations that grace the making of a work of art. Conventional films are a matter of realizing a clean, preconceived design; Bresson warns himself to be prepared for the unexpected and to bend with it so that it can be incorporated into the living texture of the work. Let no classic or perfect images draw attention to themselves; let no editing structure rationalize and clarify motivations; let not the actors think through their roles. Rather, all should happen with the smooth unrolling of a natural gesture, but a gesture acquired only after infinite, patient practice. And may this gesture be prepared to seize whatever sparks of life or truth emerge from the encounter with the subject. This is the attitude with which he made *Diary of a Country Priest.*

CRITICS have responded to this film with trepidation. Given Bresson's working methods and conception of the work of art, standard film analysis seems ludicrously inappropriate. Bazin was fully aware of this when he offhandedly outlined a conventional iconographic overlay on the film, treating it Christologically as a series of Stations of the Cross:[13] the curé's fall, the wiping of his face by Seraphita, his glorious ride on the motorcycle which delivers him to the city where he will die. In Lille he has his Gethsemane in a small café and his Golgotha in an attic room where he expires between two outcasts.

[13] Bazin, *What is Cinema?*, p. 135.

Bazin outlines but refuses to pursue this approach, finding it at best trivial, for *Diary of a Country Priest* succeeds not as an allegory of spiritual experience but as a direct exemplification of such experience. It is not, Bazin implies, a film to read so much as one to feel directly. If we must interpret it, we must do so as we interpret a song cycle by Poulenc or a group of paintings by Rouault. Though their subject matter may be conventional, all three artists are out to do something quite unconventional. They hope to create an experience inspired by the subject.

Obviously, from this aesthetic, fidelity to the subject dwindles in importance and Bresson could, without any sense of irony and in full good faith, chop forty-five minutes from his movie to satisfy the distributor. The sections cut invariably involved additional space and characters: more contact with the parishioners, the tense meeting early on with the curé superior, the extensive and grotesque consultation with Dr. Lavigne during which, amid ravings about God and morphine, the curé learns of his cancer. Bresson could cut these scenes in good faith because the essence of the film was an interior drama and rhythm, something pulsing like the diary itself beneath every image. This he produced most prominently in the least spectacular, least "cinematic" episodes. The only necessary image, as Bazin point out, was the final one, the cross toward which a life had aimed. How that life reached its final passion was not a product of tightly interlacing actions but was achieved instead by an orientation (progressively intensified, to be sure) within each episode. Albert Béguin claimed that this orientation

> from its first image to its last is the austerity of an exclusively supernatural drama. Everything in the film takes on power through the supernatural. Even the rapport between characters becomes meaningful only in terms of salvation and perdition and in terms of a community of hope.[14]

[14] Albert Béguin, "Bernanos dans le cinéma," *Esprit* 19 (1952), 248-52 (my translation).

Bresson doesn't argue for the presence of the supernatural in his film, nor does he demonstrate it as the logical result of his intrigue. It simply is there as an effect of the text, produced, critics seem to agree, by an accumulative method which couldn't be further from conventional dramatic plotting. There is no equation whereby the accidents of appearances are transformed into the necessities of plot. Rather, through repetitions of scenes, gestures, sounds, lighting, and decor, a musical rhythm invades the images, producing a meditation, with themes and variations, on the supernatural. The themes are constant and well known; the variations include dialogues, monologues, landscapes, gestures, scenes of action, scenes of writing, natural sounds, and composed music. In this way Bresson reproduces Bernanos's stunningly innovative compositional principles. For *Diary of a Country Priest* is a novel whose intense unity of concern and effect is achieved without chapters and by an amalgamation of brief acts, reflections, speeches, and descriptions. Bresson could afford to exclude and reduce the episodes because he had matched the diary form, a heterogeneous form in which tone and direction obviously take precedence over logic and completeness.

BRESSON'S *Diary of a Country Priest* is a meditation that forces us to reevaluate experience. It refuses conventional values (what counts as success in life or in cinema) and concentrates new facts and events, overdetermining them until they form a spiritual economy. The currency in this economy has many denominations (light, speech, sounds, facial expressions, simple objects, simple actions), but all are based on the same standard: the soul of the curé of Ambricourt.

In this regard the actual diary is both the film's capital and its ledger, where mundane events are invested and calculated. Or, to change to an image favored by Henri Agel, here is the heart of the film circulating the images like blood, which flows into and out of it.[15]

---

[15] Henri Agel and A. Ayfre, *Le Cinéma et le sacré* (Paris: Editions du Cerf, 1961), p. 34.

The diary is represented in three different ways in the film: as written pages on the screen, as a voice that situates the actions we see on the screen, and as those actions themselves when, through fades, ellipses, and the like, we realize that what is represented is a reflection upon an event, not the event itself.

Generally, Bresson alternates action and reflection, image and script, or image with voice. Toward the film's end, however, he insists more than ever on the interiority of all action by doubling and even trebling the signifiers of mediation. Sitting bereft at the café in Lille, trying to fathom the enormity of the death sentence he has just received, the curé turns to his diary. We watch him write. We hear him say "I must have dozed off for a while" as we see him lean back and close his eyes. A dissolve to a minutely different camera angle embodies the startled displacement he experiences in voice-over: "I must have dozed off a while. . . . [dissolve] When I awoke; Oh God, I must write this down. . . ." And as he bends forward once again over his diary, we realize he is writing the very episode we have just seen. It is a daring layering of all three modes of reflection in a single moment, concentrating our imagination with his as he conjures up the past and tries to give it a place in the story of his spiritual life.

> I think of those mornings, those last mornings of mine this week, the welcome of those mornings—the cocks crowing. That high window, so peaceful, full of night as yet, but one pane, always the same one, the right one, would begin to light up.[16]

This is his Gethsemane, and in it his face goes pale. His diary has cost him his blood, abstracted his life, and converted its acts and times to a final time—the climbing of the attic steps, the inevitable death.

By treating the diary as one object among other objects (lamps, wine bottles, prayer books, furniture), Bresson capi-

---

[16] Bernanos, *Diary of a Country Priest*, p. 225.

talizes on cinema's indifferent attachment to the physical world, only the better to set off the task of the spiritual—the transformation of physical appearance into interior value, into writing and reflection [3]. The method and goal of this process become most visible in those moments when this sublimation runs into difficulty, failing to transform or abstract certain events. Both the curé and the film find moments of death especially indigestible. As a limit to life, death is a limit to reflection as well.

Dr. Delbende's suicide is an event so difficult for the priest to absorb that he nearly destroys his diary in reflecting upon it. Death arrests him elsewhere too. A slow tilt down his desk to the open diary shows the ink still wet over the words "The countess died last night." Meanwhile, we hear his feet clattering down the steps and away into the night. In the final episode, of course, it is the dropping of the diary and the pen that signals the hour of his death.

It is at this final moment that Bresson daringly sublimates, in a single gesture, the entirety of his film. As Bazin notes, the transmutation of the diary into the images of the cross at the end, "as awkwardly drawn as on the average memorial card, is the only trace left by the 'assumption' of the image, a witness to something the reality of which is itself but a sign."[17] To return to the analogy of economics, the cross is the film's ultimate reward, a life's reward after its images, accumulated and invested with such care, have been cashed in to redeem their share of the spiritual standard that gave them value.

Bresson's task was not to explain the cross, or even the curé's relation to it, but to embody the experience of a life that terminates with the cross. Bresson here has purified the project of the novel by becoming as meek and single-purposed as its hero. Whereas Bernanos gleefully sets up a dialectic between the curé and the "dead souls" of his parishioners, a dialectic brought into focus by the curé of Torcy, Bresson never modulates his tone. The parish is judged obliquely if at

---

[17] Bazin, *What is Cinema?*, p. 141.

all by the curé's "faithful eyes," illuminated in their turn by the secret of prayer and poverty, a "lost secret" which surfaces time and again on his face.

Diary of a Country Priest has appealed to believers and unbelievers alike because it doesn't set belief in a larger context (sociological, psychological, historical). The cross, the measure of the priest's life, is itself left unmeasured. The secret may be lost for us and the cross totally discredited in our own lives or culture; nonetheless, it can be received as the only proper end to the film of this country priest.

The film's nonsectarian success testifies to the consistent and radical interiority attained by Bresson. From first to last (from the image of the diary to that of the cross) we are locked within a particular sensibility, a state of being, a soul. Bernanos struggled to render this soul, succeeding only by contrasting its meekness with the powerful, garrulous curé of Torcy, the cantankerous spokesman (so like Bernanos himself) of the public Church, of politics, and of survival. Bresson, as we have seen, pared down the novel by cutting off its public half. He bored straight to the center of the curé, where he was temperamentally at home, and from there he refused to budge. His earlier films had balanced an obsessive moral concern with (and within) a brittle and abstracted social world, but Diary of a Country Priest sees the world from a changeless point of view. There is no dialectic; all is soul.

BAZIN always claimed that style is primarily a pattern of selection. In Bresson, what pattern produces the interiority we feel? What style becomes a *particular* interior? First of all, a rigorous delimitation of means permits only certain forms and objects to be put into play: the brows, the eyes, the hands, and the feet of the characters; the thin roads and barren trees of the Calais landscape [4]; the fireplaces, doors, windows, and lamps of the dwellings; the chairs, books, and wine bottles within those dwellings. A simple iconographic deciphering of these items succeeds all too quickly in abstracting a spiritual universe while failing to touch the body of the film which these elements help constitute. It is not so much the restricted number of photographed things as the obsessive quality of the photography itself which makes of these surfaces an inner economy as well as the actual pieces of the curé's world.

One critic[18] has gone so far as to compare Bresson's photography to the Port Royal paintings of Philippe de Champaigne, with their precise hierarchy of visage over context and their spiritual clarification of authentic landscape. The inadequacy and wrongheadedness of this comparison results from Bresson's fully modernist conception of space and symbol. Space is something only suggested in his films. It is without solidity or boundaries; it expands and contracts in response to the diary. It is a fully interior space. Similarly, if symbolism is an excess of signification over the presentation of an object or scene, Bresson's film is rife with a symbolism of the second degree. We must go not only beyond the surfaces of the visible but beyond all conventional symbolic readings to attain a sense of the possibilities of the objects and events presented.

Bresson's style is haunting because it is more than a documentary of a spiritual situation and more than a cultural presentation of such a situation (in the manner of the cinema of quality and the paintings of Philippe de Champaigne); it is in fact an unstable image he gives us, in which the visible seems on the verge of rendering the invisible.

The dialogue with Chantal in the confessional is emblematic in this regard. In a single shot we move in from the opposition of two faces to concentrate on a single face in the darkness [1, 2]. Three shot-reaction shot couplets (each tightening in on the curé's brow) lead to the crisis of the letter. A single shot drops from Chantal's face to her hand, which pulls an envelope out of the darkness and joins the curé's hand in exchange. Refusing to cut, Bresson then pulls back to the initial composition of the scene and from this vantage point frames Chantal stepping forward and then out of the frame. The curé's face, on which both trauma and thanksgiving can

[18] René Briot, *Fiche Filmographique*, No. 117 (n.d.), p. 4.

be seen, immediately dissolves into the flames of the fire that consumes the sealed note. We can read through this style—we can in fact directly experience within it—the drama of two strong souls in moral combat; but far more striking is the quality of the images on which this drama rests: the darkness couching a suicide letter, rendering up a document of hate, and the luminosity of two faces and two hands in a space where voice and intention are all that count.

Similarly, the cloudy wine, particularly when it runs in pools on the floor, immediately recalls the blood of Christ, but far more interesting is its graphic relation to the "spongy" atmosphere of the landscape in general, to the mud in the fields where Dr. Delbende is found shot to death, to the mud and blood spattered on the curé's face after his hemorrhage [5]. In other words, the physical sensation of the wine flows beyond its symbolic denotation to become part of the spiritual landscape of the present—literally what he sees and senses as he acts and reflects. The moist thickness of that background retards clear vision, slows locomotion, leaves traces and stains. This graphic quality is equivalent to Bernanos's thickly adjectival style, and it operates in the film to sully any impulse to easy moral and graphic clarity.

The objects that delimit the scope of the curé's interior world are thus inseparable from the light that renders the quality of that world. Light is an explicit metaphor in the curé's discourse as he passes fearfully dark nights and comes into the sweetness of dawn. He is sensitive to the special luminescence or umbrage on each countenance he meets, and he is drawn to the warmth of fires, lamps, and windows.

Even when light is not the subject of his reflections, it colors the events he records in a formative way. At the countess's wake, for instance, mourners and family members pass him on the stairs like fleeting shadows. They form an indistinct backdrop against which he kneels by her brightly lit and flowered deathbed. More often, the subdued interiors of large flat gray walls and darker rectilinear woodwork and furniture are brightened only by areas of moderate but solid light cast by a lamp or window. The curé's face is then the site of a diagonal border between light and gray, even while it stands out against its somber context. Nothing could be further from the cinema-of-quality style with its penchant for mirrors, crystal, and a delightful mottling of a high-key world. The interiors of *Diary of a Country Priest*, on the contrary, seem to absorb much of the available light, creating a continuously dull atmosphere broken up by objects or the shadows of objects.

If the night and dawn sequences are "metaphoric" and the general flat grays are "atmospheric," we must apply the term "dramatic" to Bresson's use of source lighting. Lanterns, lamps, and flickering fires suggest at key moments the soul's resources in a dark universe [6]. In contrast, lighted windows in the night suggest the homelessness of this soul. Altogether, then, Bresson paints with several styles of lighting, but none of them is conventional. By quality standards, the ubiquitous gray geometry of light is dull and abstract while the sensual use of source lighting is too stark, especially as it fails to highlight the four corners of the screen or give a halo to crucial faces and objects. Light in these scenes is its own object—not a clarifying medium but a substance surrounded by darkness.

Despite this overall importance of light, only rarely does a single image have full pathetic reverberation, containing the spiritual state of the curé. His fall in the mud with a huge, misshapen tree trunk bisecting the screen and forming an angle with the slanted ground is one such "pictorial" exception. The self-consciously beautiful desolation of this landscape is at odds with the dominant graphic style, a style whose function is to throw the curé and the viewer forward to the next image in the hope of a final satisfying light and composition. That pictorial haven is reached only in the film's final shot—the bare shadow of a cross.

This sense of homelessness, this lack of pictorial fullness, is produced narratively as well by means of the structure of entrances and exits, a structure provided for by the diary format. Episodes commonly begin with an intrusion or expedition, many offering no development other than a repetition of this soul in transit. The actual style of these entrances and exits is more remarkable than their number. The camera remains properly with the curé as he crosses a threshold or goes to meet a visitor, but the visitor's motion is most often counter to the curé's, producing a glancing effect [7, 8]. Only rarely are two people framed in stable composition: Chantal and the curé in the confessional, the curé and the countess during her confession, Torcy and the curé when the images of his life as a holy agony come to him. These crucial moments show persons locked in combat. For the rest, the curé travels obliquely through life, and we travel with him.

The knowledge he and we have is thus strictly limited. He peers out windows at a retreating Chantal or catches a glimpse in the film's first instant of the count and his mistress, Chantal's governess, turning away from our view in the sterility of their habitual embrace.

Things are perpetually accelerating away from us in this expanding universe of the curé's consciousness. No establishing shots situate the world around him. Although few subjective first-person shots imitate his optical perspective, the displacement of the images through the diary allows us to consider even the frontal shots of the curé as belonging to his perspective. It is a lonely perspective, perhaps a paranoid one. The film is filled with glance-object shots but almost no glance-glance structures. We seldom see the curé from a human perspective other than his own. Over the course of two hours this develops a most solipsistic effect, particularly for an audience accustomed to standard French films of the quality tradition. In *La Symphonie pastorale*, for instance, a film also representing the record of events via a journal, the pastor not only looks out on the world but is looked back upon from the viewpoint of every other major character. The interlocking gazes of that film construct brilliant tableaux boxed in a cinematic diorama which the viewer's gaze contains and comprehends. Bresson, in contrast, lets us look out with the curé on the fragments of his world, but when we look back at him it is only to peer more deeply inward, to watch him reflect on his limited experience. Bresson refuses to "place" him either dramatically, sociologically, or theologically. We remain within the curé's point of view or, better, within his point of reflection.

The curé and the film avoid the temptations of paranoia and solipsism primarily through the medium of sound. If our eyes are the organs of possessiveness and clarification, our ears are responsive to the messages and events of a larger world. No sights startle the curé, especially upon reflection. He kneels calmly to retrieve the medallion that the countess has hurled into the fire; he kneels just as calmly by her deathbed. But the limited character we have noted in his visual world—its restricted elements and the alternately abstract and dark light in which those elements stand out—suggests a potentially wider world that the curé cannot or will not attend to.

Sound is the reminder of that wider world, intruding as a gunshot on the curé's familiar walk. Sounds frequently anchor the abstract reflective geometry of the images, particularly in the case of carts whose wheels squeak on the periphery of so many shots, often totally out of view but noted, present to the curé. The natural sounds of feet on cobblestones, of a motorcycle, of people whispering, dogs barking, or a breeze blowing constitute the atmosphere of the existential search for grace, and they contrast to Grunenwald's musical score, which seems to wash over the entire film from the effusive moment of its end, testifying throughout that "all is grace." Bresson was soon to divest himself of the luxury of musical scores, no doubt needing to refuse the priority of the final vision over the moments leading up to it. After all, a diary isn't written with a continuous musical feeling. Its past tense (reflecting on the day's actions) is also stringently present (what will be written in tomorrow's entry is unknown today). The Grunewald score bridges all days and announces the continuity of the priest's search—announces it and harmonizes it, but must do so against the competition of the daily sounds and unexpected noises that obstruct a clear and self-possessed rendering of the world.

No other aspect of the film so thoroughly exemplifies the structured dispossession that marks both the curé's life and Bresson's treatment of it. Bresson could rightly dispense with countless episodes from the novel simply because his sound track provided that "otherness" to which the curé, even upon reflection, found it necessary to hearken, an otherness Bernanos could convey in the novel only by means of the multiplication of events and reactions to events. Through its sound track the film found a way synchronically to present, at each of its movements, the structure of the curé's world—its pastness, its responsiveness, its fidelity of attitude, its limitation of vision, its openness to a mysterious otherness, in short, its productive loneliness and suffering.

Thus, despite its apparently hermetic form, *Diary of a Country Priest* situates itself in a cosmic openness. It is a film written across the pages of a notebook, yet it is set in a field of light and sound. The concentration and discipline of the diary allow the curé to attain in his final hours a breadth of soul explicitly measured against his pathetically liberal defrocked friend. His rigorous instrument of self-knowledge—his writing—has brought him into focus with his image and, therefore, has made him one with Christ. It is through a similar textual discipline, this time of cinematic style, that Bresson can in the end reach beyond cinema and be at one with *his* subject, a novel. By going beyond cinema through cinema, he has achieved a revolution in the ethics and potential of adaptation; he has *performed* a novel in sight and sound, not capturing his subject so much as becoming it.

CHAPTER EIGHT

Realism, Rhetoric, and the Painting of History in *Henry V*

L OGICALLY or analogically, the problem of "realism" in the cinema has much in common with that of "perspective" in painting beyond even the trivial fact that cinematic images are taken through lenses based on the conquests of renaissance painters and opticians. To a modern viewer a painting's particular relation to spatial reality is a first step in locating its genre. Every painting takes some stance in regard to the ratio of scenic to scenographic space, trompe l'oeil and abstract expressionism marking that ratio's two limits.

In cinema, while no film need strive to duplicate perceptual reality, no film can avoid comparison with our sense of real space. As André Bazin so often pointed out, film, from its very birth, has enjoyed and depended on a fundamental (ontological) rapport with spatial reality. He compared this rapport to that of an asymptote,[1] able at its limit to be indistinguishable yet distinct from reality, while at the other limit able to emphasize that very distinctiveness.

Henry V, directed by Lawrence Olivier in 1944, describes the full asymptotic curve of this relation and is, for that reason alone, a film worthy of close study. The fact that it manages to create a single, unified effect despite its stylistic (and ontic) heterogeneity makes it all the more attractive as a test case in the investigation of the status and rules of cinema among the arts.

The rhetoric of *Henry V* can first of all teach us about the rhetoric of the image. One can scarcely designate a film more

[1] André Bazin, *What is Cinema? II*, trans. Hugh Gray (Berkeley and Los Angeles: University of California Press, 1971), p. 82.

openly complicit with the prevailing ideology, dedicated as it was to the British troops and the Allied enterprise in France. Yet its complicity is so apparent, its rhetoric so conspicuous, that it makes us question the relations of cinema to social structure. Lately we have assumed that the cinema of the forties passed itself off unquestioningly as reality and we have been clever at catching this cinema out, exposing its little tricks and illusions.[2] But *Henry V* announces its artifice in countless ways: by its poetry, its colors, its sets, and of course by its "stagy" opening and close, in which the position of the audience is explicitly inscribed in the scenic space of the movie.

The film dares one to ask "What is Cinema?" as it presents us with a variety of visual and dramatic styles, succeeding one another in great blocks linked by gloriously visible transitional devices. Yet I want to argue that the film has structured these blocks so as to present us with the strongest possible illusion of the incorruptibility of the film image; this in turn founds the film's presentation of Shakespeare and the history he treats as equally incorruptible, equally bound to the "nature of things."

The structure we are speaking of is that of the hyperbola. The various narrative segments of *Henry V* occupy successive points on Bazin's asymptotic curve and achieve a hyperbolic form with the vertical axis serving as a definition of the fully real. The film moves from a most stylized, unnatural opening toward the cinematic glory of the battle of Agincourt, thence again to the precious artificiality of its concluding scenes[1-8]. Such a structure reassures the spectator with the rational symmetry of its form while constructing the central illusion of moving or peering toward something real, as down a tunnel. This something, which is glimpsed though never fully attained, is the solid action of a full-fledged battle given body through

<hr/>

[2] See especially Raymond Bellour, "The Obvious and the Code," *Screen* 15, no. 4 (Winter 1974/75), pp. 7-16. Also "John Ford's Young Mr. Lincoln," in *Movies and Methods*, ed. Bill Nichols (Berkeley and Los Angeles: University of California Press, 1976), pp. 493-528. Pam Cook, "The Duplicity of *Mildred Pierce*," in *Woman in Film Noir*, ed. E. Ann Kaplan (London: British Film Institute, 1978).

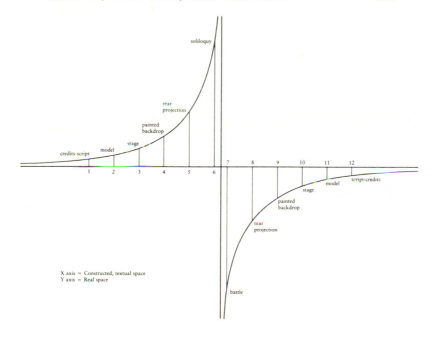

full cinematic representation, an incontrovertible event found-ing the film's more abstract notions of history, historical drama, and adaptation. It is represented, this battle, in the full per-fection of deep focus, mobile technology, an incontrovertible force of cinematography founding every sort of graphic ar-tiface and every humanization of the image which the film, in its other sections, takes such pleasure in displaying.

Let us examine this structure in detail. The symmetry of the play *Henry V* has been multiplied by the film in many ways. Not only are there the two battles (Harfleur and Agin-court), the two courts (British and French), the two scenes of soldiers bragging (the four British officers at Harfleur, the four French nobles at Agincourt); not only is there the built-in symmetry of the commoners' lives (Pistol leaving England with vows of heroism and Pistol leaving France with vows of ve-

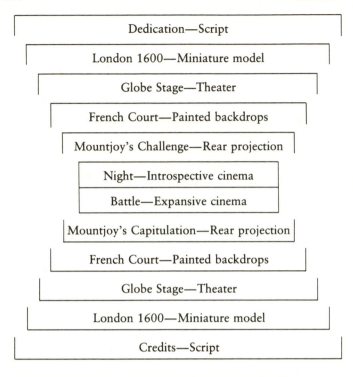

Dedication—Script

London 1600—Miniature model

Globe Stage—Theater

French Court—Painted backdrops

Mountjoy's Challenge—Rear projection

Night—Introspective cinema

Battle—Expansive cinema

Mountjoy's Capitulation—Rear projection

French Court—Painted backdrops

Globe Stage—Theater

London 1600—Miniature model

Credits—Script

nality), but the film encloses all this in a memorable bracket structure. Opening and closing with the great trip across the Thames to the theater, the action is further bracketed by the glimpse we are given at both beginning and end of the business of putting on a play. Further in, through sleight of hand, this stage turns to screen and then back again. More specifically, the tricks of model-work and the exposed tricks of the stage give way to (and later return from) the stylized decor of the courts and fields of France, where more realistic acting plays on brittle cultural sets.

We can imagine the film to have encased its treasured moments in the depths of this structure. Thus, it is only with Mountjoy's challenge to Henry and the retreat toward Calais that both image and sound render Shakespeare according to the codes of cinematic realism, yet this Mountjoy scene and his capitulation at the end of the battle are played in front of "realistic" rear projections or backdrops. They are, in other words, transitional episodes between the artificial sets of the castle and the location shooting of the battle. The battle itself sums up years of film history in the grandeur of its mise-en-scène, in the depth of its images, and in the sharpness of its montage. It is cinema's contribution (and tribute) to a dramatic text which as a verbal form could only play at the edges of the spectacular, could only invite its audience to imagine the swelling conflict. The visual excess of the filmed battle, however, runs to nearly twenty minutes while containing only a few lines of dialogue. Nevertheless, like language, it too is put at the service of the king; for however expansive the battle may be, there is little doubt that it has been well orchestrated and less doubt who its conductor is.

The montage seems the work of Harry's hands, as is the mise-en-scène. At its climax, in his personal struggle with the Constable of France, he finally plants himself in the center of this deep space and throws his last opponent. His eyes can then command the field and force the retreat of the cowardly French. The field that frightened him and his men in the dark is now possessed by his vision. From here we can return to the stylized miniature sets; from here the narrative can return to its confident representation of British character in action, based on traditional motifs.

Although the battle too echoes certain paintings (Uccello, most notably), it is primarily a cinematic conquest rather than a reproduction of an artistic conquest. That is, it absorbs the great film battles of the past (from *Cabiria* through *Alexander Nevsky*) and does them one better. For in nearly every category of cinematic expression it blares its realism and breadth. Graphically it provides us with the film's first use of unbalanced diagonals. Spears, defense pikes, and lines of troops point expansively off screen to the next shot and to further space. These are the "vasty fields of France" which Chorus dares us in his prologue to imagine. We can now measure the journey made to this broad space from the floating piece of paper announcing the play, across a model of old London and into the enclosures of the Globe. Even the more natural Boar's Head scenes are boxed in a stage space and, of course, the Duc de Berri sets, for all their play with angles, emphasize the closed and tidy world of the "miniature," in contrast to the dynamic grandeur of Agincourt.

In addition to graphic realism, natural light on the battlefield at last equalizes the colors of the film which until this moment have been so carefully segregated and ranked. Under the high sun and on the green-brown expanse of French earth (or Irish, to specify the shooting location) the cultural signification of Royal red (British) and Royal blue (French) must mix at last with the impure hues of the common soldiers, the horses, and the land at large.

The same holds true for the sound track. Outdoors at last, the music of Shakespeare's verse and Walton's score must contend with a sudden multiplicity of sound sources. Hoofs prancing, soldiers randomly shouting, the clash of axe and armor, and the whirr of arrows muddy the clean lines of a sound track which previously had encased the Bard's precious words in a cushion of music or sound-stage silence. While containing nothing like the daring cacaphony and muted speech of Welles' *Chimes at Midnight*, Olivier's battle stands out in the context of his film for the kinds and number of sounds it ushers in.

All these aspects (graphics, light, color, sound) prepare us for the two overwhelming attributes of the battle: space and movement. From the two-dimensional placard, to the box of the stage, to the miniature sets in France, and even the rear-projected studio scene with Mountjoy, we can let our eyes at last flow into a space that is as deep and clear as you like. Olivier took pains to emphasize this shift, frequently placing a character or prop (a sword stuck in the ground, for instance) in the first plane beyond which we can see tiny figures in focus nearly to the horizon line.

Now in exhilarated response to such openness the camera

frees itself from the rigid squares it has troubled to compose thus far and glides a half mile over the countryside to follow the charge. All these elements and effects cannot help but alter the viewer's relation to the film. Our initial status as grammar school pupil becomes that of the appreciative theater spectator with the aid of the on-screen Globe audience, and of the stagy acting in the French court where the sets are aimed directly, patronizingly, at us. But in the battle we feel that we are at last forgotten and must scan this space for ourselves. The only traditionally cinematic moment in what is otherwise a cultural parade, a masque, the scenes at Agincourt restore to the viewer a sense of "movie life," of watching life as given through film. Here the hyperbola comes nearest the axis of realism.

I HAVE described the battle as being lodged in the very center of the work and yet it would seem more accurate to suggest that at the center of the film is the core of Shakespearean verse, a text so solid, so incorruptible, so fructifying that it can sustain every sort of visual excess. The cinematic flourishes of the battle of Agincourt are thus driven by the dynamo of a text. Olivier insists on this hierarchy, providing as primary site for the text Shakespeare's wooden O, the Globe theater. The film, humble servant of the text, seems merely to respond to Chorus's bidding that we let our imaginations take us to France. And the eclecticism of visual styles that "imagine" the play are tribute to that which is universal but never eclectic: Shakespearean verse. The play itself, its script, holds within it all moods, so that it can embrace the successive use of styles Olivier feels free to overlay upon it.

If the battle proceeds with full visual abandon at the center of the film it is only because at the heart of the battle is the rhetoric of the St. Crispin's Day speech. Indeed Olivier's decision to photograph the heroic speeches with a retreating camera finds its full purpose here. For Henry's sureness of soul emanates to greater and greater numbers as his voice grows in amplitude and pitch. Soon he holds sway over his entire army and, as the crane shot so eloquently tells us, over the battlefield as well. The muscular battle is only a response to the unbridled verbal power of the Crispin speech.

But let us not stop short. Henry's political victory at the play's end depends upon his military victory at Agincourt and that in turn rests on the rhetorical victory over his subjects. But whence the unquestioned power of this rhetoric if not in a primary victory over self? Henry's night walk in disguise, his argument on equal footing with common soldiers, and especially his self-wrestling in soliloquy all precede (and necessarily precede) his humble prayer to his "God of Battles" and his prideful plea to his men of war.

And so, the dynamo powering the battle (and thus the entire film) is Henry's voice-over meditation on kingship and ceremony, a moment Olivier has once again charged with special significance through a peculiar strength of his medium, the strength of cinematic concentration. This stylistic strategy supports and permits its inverse, the violently expended cinematic energy of the battle.

Its opposite in every particular, this soliloquy nonetheless shares with the battle the privilege of being tied in a special way to the traditional glory of the cinema. Where the battle is expansive, the soliloquy is intensive; where the battle is bright, colorful, and full of motion, Henry's face is given as a white form on pitch black, never flinching at our long gaze. The soliloquy has a single focus and solitary object. All sounds are hushed. The voice we hear comes from off-camera as if this face before us were bodiless. The most spectacular of artforms, the cinema strives here to be the most intimate and psychological. As Bazin preached, the askesis of cinema can be, and here is, the very essence of cinema.[3]

The juxtaposition of these two inversely cinematic scenes multiplies their effect and makes Agincourt the dramatic center of the work. This is the hyperbola's moment of "singularity," as it leaps the axis from one extreme of realism to its

---

[3] André Bazin, *What is Cinema?*, trans. Hugh Gray (Berkeley and Los Angeles: University of California Press, 1967), p. 141.

equally realist opposite. All else in the film is splendor, spectacle, and celebration at which we marvel and applaud from
our seats. But at Agincourt, from the moment the camera
begins to track with (and as) Henry, we feel the ethos of the
film change and with it our role, for we are taken within a
space of existential uncertainty.

At Agincourt we run up against the film's dramatic "limit,"
the limited view accorded by the darkness, the limited perspective of Henry himself, the limitless night that so frightens
the boy. Here the film runs down to its moment of absolute
stillness. The splendor of color, of action, of history all fade
before the eternal questions Henry poses to himself. The cinema stops. The poetry comes from off-screen. As the sun
reveals, layer by layer, the battlefield of the day, so Henry's
inner discourse begins to shine publicly on his troops. It were
as if the St. Crispin's Day speech began in Henry's heart,
unheard during the night, and, amplified by prayer and meditation, could spew itself further and further out, encompassing his frightened men until they feel themselves tied to his
dream and to the power of his mission. The battle sequence,
then, is only the other side of the coin; it is cinema's reaction
to the soliloquy and the speech it gave rise to. Having con-
quered the silence of the night and the rumor of doubt, Olivier
can now let the wild horses of cinema run loose, clearing more
and more terrain under the name of Shakespeare, all with
scarcely a line of dialogue recited.

To recapitulate: the elaborate narrative and visual treatment that makes this film a spectacle rests on a core of cinematic realism; yet the realism of space on Agincourt's battlefield is already dependent on an earlier and deeper moment,
the stillness of Henry's meditation. At the core of history, the
film tells us, is the power of the great man, a power of self-
mastery generating crowd mastery and the mastery of the
future. It is through the systematic denial of visual excess,
through the subsumption of the image to the spirit in Henry's
Gethsemane, that all visual excess is justified.

WHAT is the force of a term such as "spirit" in this framework?
Even to the moment of death the sick person feels somewhere
within a sustaining core, what some have called "soul." The
seat of all force when we are healthy, it is to this core that,
delirious, we retreat when ill. Not just a force, it is a place,
a shiftless position on which we fight our battles. The body
gets leverage from this position when it is beleaguered from
without; the body returns to this place as refuge when illness
corrupts from within. For that inner core, in both sinner and
saint, is the place of continuity, the guarantee of selfhood.

It was this core that Freud suggested would become the
subject of a new and radical doubt,[4] triggered by a new and
radical disease, mental illness, the fission of the soul under
pressure from something more basic, that which Freud termed
"the indestructible," the unconscious and its instincts. Among
other things, literature is a representation of this core in action.
Generally the soul stands up against other souls seeking its
proper or improper position in a field of action. Epic especially
observes and narrates this total positioning. Drama more commonly represents a moment of crisis in which a core is exposed.

Freud found that of all dramatists Shakespeare most fear-
lessly put the soul itself in question, representing not just the
struggle of a soul in a field of others but the struggle of a soul
to retain its unity against those darker forces which split it
into moods, personae, voices of the self. While twentieth-
century performances of Shakespeare have accentuated this
modernism of his art, Olivier's *Henry V* renders a Shakespeare
we are comfortable with, one who is never more reassuring
than here. Olivier's Shakespeare ordains the social order by
founding it firmly on a king's super-soul and then protecting
it within history, within the borders of a painterly space, and
within the warm cushioning music of William Walton.

But the drama in this film remains a drama for all that; and

[4] Sigmund Freud, *On Creativity and the Unconscious* (New York: Harper
& Row, 1958), p. 6.

this feeling of comfort, an effect of the rhetorical organization of moral and pictorial space, is something that needs to be achieved in a field of danger and in a scenario of threats overcome. Although Freud was alluding primarily to the tragedies, one can sense Shakespeare's concern about fragmentation in his histories as well. Often the leader of the state or the villain who covets high position is made to go through an extraordinary moment of self-doubt comparable in tone to that of Hamlet or Lear. Olivier's treatment of Henry's soliloquy before the battle is an "existential" reading of the character of Henry, indebted to our general sense of the tragic Shakespearean soliloquy. Moreover Shakespeare's concern with psychic disease and dispersal can be said to extend in the histories beyond the personality of a national leader to the state itself.

Such political uses of personal dramatic struggle were well known to him. From Plato's image of the charioteer reigning in wild horses, the state has always been seen as analogous to the beleaguered soul. In moments of crisis or doubt the analogy can be dramatized so all can recognize that the innate sanctity of the soul struggling with itself or others must be accorded to the state as well, especially in its quest to outlast turpitude, rebellion, or war.

In his histories, Shakespeare was at pains to prove the right of a new politics of will, a right reflected in the hierarchic structure of British society, rooting Elizabeth and her subjects in a medieval past, with its divine right of monarchy. Olivier, for his part, is at pains to connect his battered London of 1944 to the London of the Bard, the core of the culture. Shakespeare lodges the life of the state within one man, powerful enough to lead a nation, human enough to understand his subjects. Olivier lodges the life of the state further down, within the molecular makeup of the king, in the psychological balance he exhibits. For Olivier and for us the king is not some individual privileged by birth to lead, but a human being, like us, who leads, as we might, on the strength of his moral and psychic well-being. Common sense is one name for this strength, common sense, the national moral attribute of England. In this way Olivier gives to his country in 1944 a play that presents the hints of a modern problem (weakness of purpose, self-doubt, the splitting of the psyche) and the relief of a modern solution (the king as everyman or, at least, every Englishman), all boxed within layer upon layer of celebratory wrapping.

OLIVIER'S strategy of layering derives its authority from Shakespeare himself who encased a serious tone within the pageantry of his histories. Where Shakespeare found himself rectifying the events and demands of two ages, his own and that of the early fifteenth century, Olivier must juggle the concerns of three. His handling of the Shakespearean original in terms of textual fidelity and graphic context reveals the method and function of this layering, just as a study of Shakespeare's use of Holinshed's Chronicles provides access to the Elizabethan appropriation of the past.

I leave it to Shakespeare scholars to establish and definitively rectify the texts.[5] We need only note the elimination of intranational conflict at Southhampton, as well as many speeches manifesting Henry's unbridled bragging, his thrusts of cruelty, and his theological justifications for the war. These would have blocked a modern audience from the full respect the play demands he be given, and so these were among the first of the 1,600 lines to be cut.

More interesting is the inclusion of Falstaff's deathbed dialogue with Hal, transported here from *Henry IV, Part II*. No doubt Olivier and his text editor Robert Dent were eager to give a mass audience some toehold in this remote play, and Falstaff might well be thought of as a national hero far more endearing than King Henry himself. But the manner of its presentation marks Falstaff's death with special rhetorical significance and requires closer analysis. Just before we cross the

[5] Harry Geduld, *Film Guide to Henry V* (Bloomington: University of Indiana Press, 1973), pp. 47-58.

Channel to the effete French court and just after we have left the Globe, the camera on its own creeps up to Falstaff's chamber and climbs through the window into the warm light of the room. There we hear Falstaff pleading for the new-crowned king to recognize him and we hear the fatal rebuke, "I know thee not, old man." All this comes to us from the utter stillness of the room. A voice (off-screen) emanates through the screen of history; the earlier play wells up and has its impact on the surface of this one.

The interior voice of Henry conquering the dying voice of Falstaff establishes that core of kingly strength which it was the point of the Henry IV plays to question and then to reveal. Falstaff's death leaves the commoners weak, for they now have lost their prince of weakness. Ironically they must follow the very Henry whose refusal of Falstaff caused his death. The camera looks back up at this death room as the sequence ends, noting the closing of the window, the snuffing of the lamp. This room of warmth has now become the coffin of Sir John, cold echo chamber of Hal's voice. If the Globe theater is the omphalos of the film, the Boar's Head is the space in England with central moral sanctity. Neither literal theater, nor the theater of the court, it is the human measure of a king and his subjects.

Graphically Falstaff's death copies Dutch paintings a half century nearer us than Shakespeare. The Vermeer setting with its single light source warming the profile of Mistress Quickly silences the scene in that "suspension" Huizinga wrote about, "Everything in Vermeer . . . lies in suspension, as it were, an atmosphere of childhood recollection, a dream-like peace, a complete stillness, an almost elegiac clarity which is too refined to be described as melancholy."[6] But others have called it melancholy, a "melancholy sense of the passage of time, of all that escapes with the vanishing moment, the hours slipping inexorably by with the sun and the light on the wall, the

[6] Johan Huizinga, *Dutch Civilization in the Seventeenth Century*, trans. A. Pomerans (New York: Ungar, 1968), pp. 84-85.

disappearing day, the already visible shadow."[7] In Falstaff's room we find as well the gentleness of approach that savors the dying light in all its beauty, rescuing it through the work of the camera. It will remain for us an image of a warmly domestic England that can stand up against the brightly illuminated and noble settings of courtly France. [Frontispiece]

Falstaff's death scene, a still picture bearing the weight of serious dramatic energy, rhymes with Henry's midnight soliloquy at Agincourt. In both, the voice-over technique charges a quiet image with history and import. The image in the latter scene is once again Northern European in origin, the first return to this style since the death of Falstaff. It is prepared for by an elaborate itinerary making it possible for a public king to leave his public decor and, disguised, search out the lights of his common soldiers, the conversations of their campfires. The darkness surrounding the campfire, where the boy's intense honesty of face belies the king's clichés, brings us not into the world of Vermeer but into that of Rembrandt. This is a psychological space, and the soliloquy, as we have seen, confirms it.

The use of Rembrandt lighting in this sequence is not nearly so precious as the other painterly allusions in the film. Recall that, along with the battle which follows it, this is the film's most naturally cinematic sequence. Yet this admission only points to a truism about film lighting: namely, that since 1920 Rembrandt has been the cinema's dominant model.[8] Frankly the lighting in this scene goes beyond Rembrandt in its romanticism and, as Harry Geduld notes, concludes with touches which border on the pre-Raphaelite.[9] Nevertheless, this style of lighting is a conventional signifier of a mysterious or psychological space in the cinema. It marks, therefore, the film's most immediate moment, the point at which this pageant takes

[7] René Huyghe in *La Poetique de Vermeer* (1948) cited in V. Block, *All the Paintings of Jan Vermeer* (New York: Hawthorne, 1963), pp. 46-47.

[8] See, for instance, Charles G. Clarke, *Professional Cinematography* (Hollywood: American Society of Cinematographers, 1964), p. 115.

[9] Geduld, *Film Guide to Henry V*, p. 60.

on the grand seriousness dark movies customarily involve. Just as the commoners' scenes were modern in Shakespeare's day, so this scene has been modernized for us.

The scenes of Falstaff's death and of Henry's soliloquy stand out as remarkable for the intimacy and depth of their presentation. They are put in relief by the more spectacular medieval compositions which make up the larger portion of the film. These sequences are based on reproductions of the *Très Riches Heures of Jean, Duc de Berri*, which Olivier had seen printed in an issue of *Verve* and determined to employ.[10] It was a daring and utterly successful decision. The manuscript is chronologically congruent with the events portrayed. More important, it lends to those events a shiny veneer that reflects back up through the centuries.

In contrast to the warm and involving coloring of the Falstaff and night pre-battle scenes, the French court is impersonal, brilliant, and brittle. Employing metals, books of hours tend to appear lit from within, the color being valuable for itself rather than depicting or fleshing out some figure. Indeed, in the original manuscripts the play with false perspective worked to counteract the horizontal and flat movement of the eye across a page of black-and-white lettering. In the film the play of color and false perspective serves as an orchestra shell for the Shakespearean verse recited against it. We admire the light and are bathed in it as the colors advance toward us, decorating the poetry that strikes our ear.

Olivier's decision to use such decor is all the more instructive when we realize that the fifteenth century marked not only the zenith of illuminated manuscript painting, but the birth of perspective and the origin of source lighting. It is this latter that finds its fulfillment, through Caravaggio (contemporary with Shakespeare), in the Dutch seventeenth century. Renaissance Netherlands prized the physicality of light, including its limitation in shadows, over against the general undifferentiated religious illumination of medieval painting.

[10] *Ibid.*, p. 19.

At the same time their subjects themselves became secularized, moving away not just from Christian *topoi*, but from mythological themes as well. Everyday people were given their moment in time and space, not sculpted as in renaissance portraiture, but in the activity of their everyday lives (reading a letter, pouring milk). Now we can see why Olivier saved this style of lighting for the commoners in Shakespeare's play. The colors here are much earthier and make us approach them, invade the picture, and feel it. The textures of the figures are suggested by the shadows which mottle even the most well lit portions of such images.

We would routinely call these images more real and more natural than those of the French court if Shakespeare himself had not questioned this very notion in the play. At the denouement, as Henry and Kate are about to entangle themselves and their nations through a highly cultivated word game, the Duke of Burgundy delivers one of the play's longest speeches. As the camera pans from his view out a window and across a landscape, he rues the state of the French countryside, "best garden of the world." The wars have left the fields abandoned to their own designs. Weeds, wild growths, and tangles have obscured the geometry men had painstakingly ordained. The country's youth has as well gone untended and exhibits instincts unthinkable in society. In summing up his plea for peace and "husbandry," he laments that everything has become "unnatural."[11]

For Burgundy the geometric designs of the landscapes in the illuminated miniatures are natural. For him the light that emanates from them and bathes us in its benevolence is a light that culture has given to the earth and that exists in France when the values of culture illuminate her. For him history and politics make the earth natural, when the king, as God's representative, circumscribes and parcels out the land with a gesture of his sceptor of peace.

But for Shakespeare the question was not so easy. Burgundy

[11] William Shakespeare, *Henry V*, Act V, sc. ii.

has but one voice in this drama. He is answered by the "more natural" voices of Falstaff and his friends for whom the instincts of survival and pleasure, tied to a vision of the king as the rampaging Prince Hal, make up a powerful antiphon. Shakespeare is not out to gainsay Burgundy and the medieval view but to give it enough renaissance body to make it come alive for his contemporaries. He is not out to denigrate King Henry but to increase his stature by giving him the flesh of his youth.

Shakespeare's work on history gives "depth" to Holinshed's Chronicles by presenting the events of the chronicle from a variety of viewpoints. Not only is there a nearly equal interplay between lords and commoners, but the latter are conscientiously divided into types and regions (Welsh, Irish, Scot, and British). The insertion of these few scenes cracks the veneer of official history and permits a vision of events involving not only the king but his subjects as well. Specifically it suggests that the state is made up of a relation between king and subjects. Thus we peer through the blocks of events in history toward the molecular structure of microevents in which everyone is engaged. To use the film's artistic allusions, the Godlike space and light of the late middle ages is broken up into the humanized space and deep shadowy light of the renaissance view.

Olivier tends to diminish the importance of intra-national tension in his filming of the play. Instead he foregrounds Henry's internal tensions. Just as Shakespeare chose certain aspects of the chronicle of the Plantagenet dynasty to emphasize in order to present not a medieval but a high renaissance picture to his audience, so Olivier has chosen to build from certain of the play's suggestions to create a picture useful to modern Britain.

The lodging of the psychological scene at the film's very center is, I think, a modern move, and one that responds to the realities of a democratic country which nevertheless is obsessed with royalty. The entire history of a nation is compressed onto a flat screen, like an accordion, until it achieves two-dimensionality graspable by the eye. But this very image, this comforting total view of history, depends upon the existential moment of Henry in the night, a moment in which (Olivier would have us believe) all the resources of technology are gone. All mediation (the cinema, the stage, the paintings, and even the action) melts away as we confront a face in meditation. Although this very askesis of technology is itself a code of inwardness (the inner voice, we might say, paralyzes our vision), it is a code we have a certain faith in. This is the film's pretense to modernism. If the film celebrates politics, civilization, valor, and the rest, it does so because at its heart it celebrates the man alone, the king who, like all of us, must work things out in the night. Of course, unlike the rest of us, this king has Shakespearean language to think with. Under the guise of a psychological problem, then, the film founds itself on the Shakespearean core and thereby conquers not only the moral problems of the single moment but the political, social, sexual, agricultural, and artistic terrain the play freely romps within.

OLIVIER'S *Henry V* is an intersection of perspectives that justify England and civilization and that call for their defense. Perspective is always the result of a conquest. The achievement of visual perspective in painting around 1400 did not occur bloodlessly. Even the illuminated drawings on which the sets were based show the traces of a struggle to present a solid against the picture plane and to tilt that picture plane against a scene so that its oblique lines could let us imagine its volume. Similarly the achievement of the history plays of Shakespeare shows a terrible struggle to rectify the chaos of events, the overturning of authority, the fickle play of morality and power; but they do achieve a perspective, a Tudor view of past and present, by ordering events in relation to the lives of key figures and groups of common subjects. The film's struggle, I am arguing, occurs only briefly in the pre-battle sequence. For, up until that moment and then again after the battle, actors, decor, music, and camera all play toward us, representing the *achievements* of language, painting, narration. But in that one sequence we can sense the struggle that precedes achievement. The bravura is gone. The music subsides. Actors play to one another and the camera works to find a truth in this drama relevant for our times. This is the attainment of psychological perspective by means of subjective camera, the reduction of spectacle, the study of faces, the voice-off, and the deep dark space crossed by flickering and intermittent campfire light. The film here struggles cinematographically with the problem of intimacy and tries thereby to give both space and history a private and personal side. This is the moment of truest drama in the film, the rest being epic representation. The audience surely feels its role shift from that of recipient to that of co-creator.

Let's use the analogy of perspective which the film so generously affords us. In the fifteenth century, depth in painting came by way of manipulating a solid body so that it appeared oblique to the picture plane. By analogy, *Henry V* belongs to a new era of adaptation where the depth of the original is suggested through the turning of the original against the screen. Of course the whole play is not given; there is always a hidden side. Of course we partake of an illusion of the original; but Olivier's *Henry V* has gained something for the cinema in suggesting the solidity of the original by turning it on its side. If we have faith in that original, if we enter the soul of Henry, then the whole experience will wash over us just as surely as a perspective painting is accepted as a three-dimensional image of its object.

In a quaint way the film alludes to the struggle of the fifteenth century to break into a deep view of space, one that would account for the point of perception. That era needed to organize geography and control it. The film includes less quaintly and more seriously the Elizabethan struggle to break into a perspectival view of events so that the fluctuating chronology of plagues, revolutions, and allegiances could be coherently organized. Most seriously of all, the film represents and embodies our own struggle to break into a psychological perspective, responding to our need to organize the self and its motivations in a larger social sphere, to connect a private and a public time and space.

The structuring of the two preconstructed worlds (the medieval, the renaissance) around the modern one rebutts the charges made against the film's apparent stylistic eclecticism. Returning to the analogy of the hyperbola we can say now that Olivier has figured in his film the *cumulative* movement of British history. By arranging his allusions and preconstructed views of history in a hyperbolic sequence he has achieved the illusion that all such constructions are ultimately based on an unconstructed point of truth.

To alter the analogy, at the center of the film is the vanishing point of real space, the full exterior space suggested by the cinematic battle, the infinitely deep interior space of the king's meditation. The cultural, artistic fashionings of the film are not diminished in contrast to this point of spatial and dramatic realism; rather they make it visible like the contructed geometry tunneling our vision through a flat painting, or like all the technological construction requisite for the capturing of real images on film. Reality is the purpose of the construction and reality guarantees the rightness of these particular fabrications. In this way both British history and British culture (Shakespeare) are confirmed sacramentally by the cinema which, while not reality itself, is reality's ordained representative in the world of art.

Through the privileged medium of reality, a time, a place, and a history are rendered comprehensible, reasonable, and worth maintaining. The film justifies this vision by resting on the language of Shakespeare, and it centers that language in the core of the film so that our acceptance of the language is at once an acceptance of the film and of the ethos of the film. This is homage, but it is homage that is useful to a time. In 1943 the English may well have retreated to their island, may indeed have retreated underground to escape the German bombers every night, but such a retreat would at last, the film proclaims, allow them to touch base with their soul. We find in this film an image of that national soul emanating ultimately from the wooden O of the Globe. England's dark night is Harry's dark night. If he was able to come through it ready for action and in touch with himself it was thanks to Shakespeare; thanks to that same Shakespeare all Englishmen will come through it all right, will feel themselves morally free, heroic, and unafraid, for they speak his language, or at least they understand it.

Through the calculated perspective of the adaptation and through the real illusion of cinematic depth, Olivier has confounded culture and nature. We travel down the opulent tunnel of this film to encounter the nakedness of man and the bare reality of language. The word is the vanishing point of this grand historical tableau and therefore the truth that legitimates the film's myriad illusions. Conversely, by bringing us self-consciously to welcome an experience of solid visible reality at Agincourt, Olivier prepares us to welcome an experience of inner reality as well, the language of the self. By joining our belief in the visible and the linguistic through the structure of layering a core, Olivier has joined as well the fragile momentary inner life of every viewer to the continuity of cultural life in history. Crucially it was the cinema that permitted this merging of perspectives, via its eclectic reproduction of painting, drama, and music, and via its unique "asymptotic" convergence on the real. Seldom has cinema participated in a more massive ideological undertaking. Seldom has it seemed, both historically and aesthetically, more worthwhile.

CHAPTER NINE

Echoes of Art:
The Distant Sounds of Orson Welles

ENTER a "body of work," a "corpus of films." Orson Welles, decadent individualist that he is, illegitimate son of European high art traditions, knew the *auteur* theory in advance and set out to make a series of films whose variety would make sense to later critics intent on their unity.

At the center of this body, then, what? A soul, a spirit, an animating force, a world view, a style? Welles' opus as well as his personality invites a descent into the core, into the heart of darkness pumping blood into the miles of images for which he has been responsible. In this, *Citizen Kane* is exemplary: a film to peel, to unlayer and explore. It is arranged in separable skins: the title, the rising camera invading Xanadu's grounds, the word "Rosebud" spoken from inside a dying man, a newsreel of his life, a series of separate interviews, a final omniscient camera summary, and the credits at the end. What is at the center of this onion? The plot reveals to us the glass ball and the sled, the privileged symbols of a man's last and, it is argued, his perpetual obsession.

Critics turn away from this "find" as "dollar-book Freud" only to posit another core, one that satisfies not the plot of Kane's past but that other plot, the one of discovery and detection, the plot of the search for Kane's past. The center of this detective tale is given and remarked upon: it is the jigsaw puzzle. No matter that it bears a meaning of failure and incoherence, the symbol itself is absolutely coherent. Planted, like the glass ball, at several points in the film, the jigsaw puzzle as explicator comes to relieve Thompson who sums up his search in a final phrase ("I guess Rosebud is a piece in a jigsaw puzzle, a missing piece") just as the name on the sled is about to be revealed, solving the question opened by the film's first word. How can we be satisfied with either?

"Rosebud," a glass ball, a sled . . . our dissatisfaction with these is our refusal of metaphor, of the single sacred signifier capable of clarifying the full life of a man. The jigsaw puzzle and the missing piece . . . our rejection of this cliché is a refusal of metonymy, of the progressive unraveling of a truth. The hollowness of both these solutions points to the hollowness of the cinema, that medium made up of image and tale, of metaphor and metonymy intermixed. Thus the film collapses under its own success, leaving us to meditate on the unrepresentable, on the mystery or emptiness of life.

Nearly all of Welles' films move like *Citizen Kane* toward cloying parables or metaphors that threaten to explain in a few words the delicious problem we expect to savor for two hours. There is the tale of the scorpion in *Mr. Arkadin*, which some critics have used to ground their sense not only of that film but of Welles and all his work. Then there is the patently oversimplified Holinshed's Chronicles providing a clear but hopelessly meager view of life in England in Falstaff's time. *The Magnificent Ambersons* moves to its denouement once Lucy can recite her parable about the sad fate of the Indian brave, Vendonah.

It is no wonder critics have credited to Orson Welles the sections of *The Third Man* in which he appears, since the film's key scene places Welles and Joseph Cotton high atop a ferris wheel where Welles as the mysterious Harry Lime can summarize the moral problem of the film in his characteristically parabolic manner ("Look down there. Would you really feel any pity if one of those dots stopped moving forever?"). The wheel itself is a complex metaphor for the action and the milieu, just the kind of temptingly explicit backdrop against which Welles could indulge his penchant for clever aphorisms. Finally, and with extreme self-consciousness, Welles (in *F for Fake*) threatens to sum up his whole career by laying out his major insights as sleight of hand. This film concludes with the extended "Picasso" parable on authenticity.

What is the function of these parables? First of all they serve as central nodes in the onion structure of the films. Dramatic resting points, they reflect back and forth across the intrigues that they directly interpret. Even as these explanations fail we sense the rightness of the attempt and we experience in the film the doubleness and distance that so define the world of Orson Welles. The parable is, in short, a peculiar but integral part in the engine of Wellesian drama.

The ostentation of aphorisms, parables, and metaphors gives to the "thought" of his films the same flamboyance that characterizes the "spectacle," to use Aristotle's language. Not only is Welles a magician in the realm of special effects, editing, and mise-en-scène, the ideas his films ask us to entertain are striking, troubling, unforgettable. And if he is subject to charges of empty bravura, of eclecticism, and even of plagiarism in his panoply of dramatic tricks, and in his parade of cinematic styles, so we must cast a skeptical eye on the "serious ideas" each film develops. The insufficiency of the parables is an index to the overall hollowness of the intellectual body of his work, to its eclecticism, to its derivative, often faddish origins. Welles organizes these ideas not for their truth or consistency but for their sheer effect. It is all dollar-book Freud, or Kafka, or Nietzsche, or Shakespeare.

And so in both its outward appearance and its inner soul *Citizen Kane* (like all his films) demands our admiration, evokes our astonishment, only to leave us with a feeling of emptiness and fraud. This is the vapidity of paradox from Zeno to Nietzsche, and Welles is only too proud to extend this tradition, adding to it the specifically illusory dimension of moving pictures.

WELLES is not the first director to express the emptiness of appearances and to question the solidity of the world or ideas he so forcefully images. As a master of the long take and the tracking camera he engages a cinematic aesthetic ruled by the great names of F. W. Murnau, Kenji Mizoguchi, and Max Ophuls. If Welles obtrudes from this company we must blame his ostentation. Next to the delicate realism of Murnau, the refined rigor of Mizoguchi, and the relentless irony of Ophuls, Welles stands out as gaudy, even inauthentic.

One is tempted to blame this on production conditions. Only his first two films approached the budget, studio support, and independence routinely accorded Murnau and Mizoguchi toward the end of their careers. But even Welles' first films exemplify a cloying cleverness that cheapens the artistry while it draws attention directly to itself. Here, despite all his efforts to mask it, Welles shows himself the quintessential American. His lack of good, or even sustained, taste gives him away, especially beside the authentically cultured Murnau, the thoroughly disciplined Mizoguchi.

Mizoguchi and Murnau spent whole lifetimes in the pursuit of a style and theme they could rely on. They studied, experimented, and repeated their experiments until they achieved a stance from which to peer out at the moral vistas that attracted them. Welles has never trusted his footing, has never struggled long enough to earn one. He expects to accomplish by cleverness and energy what others gain through artistic instinct or prodigious labor.

We have already encountered one of Welles' cleverest devices in the parable. The parable is a false discourse not only because it is a logical magic trick but because it is a set piece lodged within the very situation it purports to explain. It is a conditioned discourse posing as unconditioned truth. Welles' own relation to these "truths" is the most troubling aspect of his narrational tone. Does the magician believe in the tricks that bear away the faith of his audience? This is the subject of *F for Fake* which spoofs artistic originality.

The issue of authenticity and certitude has always been at the center of his films, as though his world view is a distrust of, or nostalgia for, integral views. Welles' parables promise integral views but come to us through the fractured prisms of his films. There may rest a truth deep in the parable but the

parable itself lies so far down in the film that we cannot reach
or listen to it directly. And the voice which speaks it so pompously does so with the echo of great distance or with the
cackle of ironic smirking.

Would Welles trade his cleverness, his ability to manipulate,
for talent or wisdom? Would he trust the perceptions arising
from either? Clearly he admires the integral vision of a Shakespeare or even an H. G. Wells; but his obsession with adaptation reveals more certainly a crisis in his own perception
and in that of his age. Never has he sought merely to reproduce
an earlier vision for our times, nor even to amend or supple-
ment the sources he admires. The original work (*The Trial,
Othello, The Magnificent Ambersons*) maintains its integrity
by virtue of tradition, by its name or that of its author, while
Welles employs it for one or more of its obvious effects. And
the employment is qualified by other effects such as acting,
lighting, sets, and camera angle which purport to deliver the
message of the original to us.

In the adaptations as in the parables, an authoritative voice
of a previously formulated truth issues from the center of the
films; and yet no voice or truth comes to us purely or directly.
Welles has caged Shakespeare, Kafka, Isak Dinesen. They are
the rabbits he conjures out of his hat. He lets us believe they
are his intimate friends whom he is generous enough to put
on display for our edification, whereas in fact he calls upon
them to remind himself of the paucity of his own vision. The
strength of their voices betrays the insecurity behind the sten-
torian style of his cinematic delivery. The power of Shakespeare, like that of Kafka's parable of the law courts, fills us
with awe, but it is a power removed from us, vitiated in the
labyrinth of the films. The flesh and blood at the center of
these films is seen only as an array of images in a hall of
mirrors, each shatterable, each but a centimeter thick.

A scheme of multiple narrators accomplishes this project
of embedding each film's values as mirages inaccessibly deep
inside the magic box of the work. Once again, *Citizen Kane*
provides the best example of this strategy. Six versions of

Kane's life are told, some of which explicitly question the possibility of a uniform or total view. The subject of these narratives and of the film as a whole, Charles Foster Kane, recedes into the center of a narrative maze; the more we search, the more paths we find we must take and the less certain we become of what we see. The giant Kane is at once magnified and dissolved by this technique: magnified as the focus of multiple views and concerns, yet dissolved into the inevitable forgetfulness of the past. He is irretrievable except in story, and every story is qualified by its neighbor.

Certainly Welles' apprenticeship in radio taught him the possibilities of the framed story, of qualifying introductions, and of nested tales. So thorough is his taste for this structure that his fullest rendition of Shakespeare, *Chimes at Midnight*, is consciously re-presented rather than directly staged for the camera. Holinshed's Chronicles set the scene but only after Falstaff and Master Shallow have stared into the camera, full of age and memory, declaring "We have heard the chimes at midnight [23]." The film might properly be thought of as a retrospective gaze.

Stephen Heath has convincingly shown[1] that the key dramatic movement in *Touch of Evil* as well as that film's central moral drama involve neither the murder during the opening credits nor Charlton Heston's search for justice, but rather concern Hank Quinlan's past, told to us in bits and fragments. The dramatic lulls in Tania's place are symptoms of the real story the film encases, that of Hank Quinlan's trauma years ago and his subsequent obsessions and decline. There at the center of the film, in a neutral, quiet spot between Mexico and America, the real tragedy is laid out to reverberate forward and back through the plot, until Tania can conclude the film with her famous line, "He was some kind of a man."

Of course, certain of Welles' films make embedded stories the very subject of their interest. One could say this of *Mr.*

[1] Stephen Heath, "Film and System; Terms of Analysis," *Screen*, 16, no. 1 (1975), 7-77.

Arkadin, which begins with a double flashback and features
a search for an event lodged years earlier still in Poland, an
event whose disclosure has the power to shatter a life and an
empire, yet an event whose real existence depends completely
on its inclusions in the stories of the past that the characters
tell each other.

In its very title *The Immortal Story* is a fable about fables.
James Naremore writes, "The film as a whole has been structured like a nest of boxes containing a story within a story
and reminding us, with constant references to Welles' previous
films, that the director himself is like Clay (the main character). Thus Welles strives to create fictions that will live,
standing outside his actors like a puppet master, always aware
of his mortality."[2] Where *F for Fake* shows all art to be
inauthentic, *The Immortal Story* shows that in the power of
artifice lies the chance for the only authenticity available to
man. Clay literally brings to life a story that no one otherwise
would believe. The intermeshing of art and illusion goes no
further in Welles' work. The fragility of appearance here attains the palpability of fact even though it is set ("nested") in
an infinite regress of tales and tellings. Man is mortal but the
lies of fiction never end. The multiple mirrors around Clay's
head at the outset of the film signal this in a single image.
Truth lies in the telling, in the reflections, rather than in the
mirage of what is there seen.

WELLES' narrational tone is one of calculated bravura. The
parables he infatuates us with are insufficient to explain the
moral situations of the films. The rhetoric of the great authors
he adapts reminds us of a seriousness and authenticity that
the films as a whole lack. At no time in all dozen films do
we feel a weakness of purpose or slovenliness of presentation.
Everything is presented as powerfully as possible, often with
a technical and stylistic flare that comes near to being haughty.

---

    [2] James Naremore, *The Magic World of Orson Welles* (New York: Oxford
University Press, 1978), p. 293.

Ultimately we are impressed by the vanity of such presentations, sickened by the emptiness of the rhetoric.

This tone of narrative voice takes its cue from the obsessive theme that dominates every film, that of disintegration. Like the structure of paradox discussed earlier, the narrative structure presents us with an impressive façade sliding into decay and oblivion. Characters, knowledge, entire ways of life are undermined and collapse over the course of his films.

This two-step method (creating an appearance of solidity, then permitting it to crumble before our eyes) is most visible in his treatment of the wax museum of characters everyone knows by heart, a museum Welles heats to the melting point: Charles Foster Kane, Hank Quinlan, Macbeth, Othello, Gregory Arkadin, Falstaff, Joseph K. It concerns as well the decline of gentility in *The Magnificent Ambersons*, of Merrie England in *Chimes at Midnight*, of rationality in *The Trial*, of storytelling in *Immortal Story* and of authorship in *F for Fake*.

Everything is made important and sacred in Welles' world only the better for him to deride the important and to question the sacred. This not only controls the overall rhythm of each scenario, it permeates the inner fabric of the mise-en-scène directing the presentation of the scenes themselves. André Bazin was the first to notice this method, coining the term "blocks of reality" to describe the molecular units at the core of *Kane* and *Ambersons*.[3] All the key scenes of *Ambersons* are rendered in single take, giving them a solidity unknown up to that time in the Hollywood cinema. Each scene, Bazin claims, is a block that stands before us with unquestionable authority. Welles' artistry consists of preparing these blocks before filming and in arranging them in a dramatic rhythm during editing. But the scenes themselves unroll of their own accord, the camera recording (rather than constructing or even representing) the scene as though it were a building or territory to be rendered. Even such a lengthy and edited sequence as that of the ball in *The Magnificent Ambersons* attains substantial body through

---

[3] André Bazin, *Orson Welles* (Paris: Editions du Cerf, 1972), pp. 62-70.

the distance of the camera, its refusal to enter the scene via cross-cutting or subjective view of any sort [13], and most memorably through the solemnity of its rhythm which out-waits the confident music of the ball, holding every shot be-yond its dramatic significance, until the characters finally re-alize that the evening is over [14]. Far from being the romantic dream of a debutante, this ball is the concrete realization of an epoch celebrating himself. Because of its density, it will later stand unforgettable as a memory node, lodged in every-one's mind, a communal image the reality and disappearance of which we have witnessed.

The inevitable dissolution across that film's range of char-acters and their way of life is only the most obvious method Welles has of tearing down what presents itself as confident. Transitions occur continually in individual scenes. The end of *Ambersons* offers a succession of devastating scenes each of which crumbles before our eyes: Isabel's carriage ride back to her home and to her deathbed in which her profile subsides into ever darker shadows [17]; Eugene's attempt to see her which is thwarted by Georgie, Fanny, and Jack standing on increasingly higher landings of the great staircase so that Eu-gene's romantic presence and straightforward good will is made ridiculous; Isabel's death rendered with the simple fall-ing of a mottled shadow across her face [18], the final curtain pulled while Georgie's silhouette turns away in sadness. Now comes the film's shortest and most experimental scene. In the darkness of an antechamber the Major pushes himself toward the camera; he turns screen right and we follow him while we hear Aunt Fanny sobbing. A figure then cuts between the camera and the Major so abruptly that we turn to follow it until Fanny whirls in from screen right to embrace Georgie coming back the other way muttering, "She loved you, George; it was you she loved." Never in the era of Hollywood cinema has a camera been so ungrounded, so at the mercy of hushed but whirling character emotions. The scene, like the charac-ters, flies away from the camera, dispersing itself so that there is nothing to hold onto, nothing to photograph. Unremittingly

Welles pursues this anxiety in the Major's mad ramblings about the origin of the world and the place of man ("The sun; it must be the sun"). Again without a cut we watch him stare blankly at us as the shadows of a fire flicker across his troubled face. Finally, as though to lighten the atmosphere, Welles gives us the parting of Jack from Georgie at the train station [19, 20]. This seemingly ordinary and obligatory scene nevertheless sustains the mood of the film by the severe manner of its presentation. Georgie utters not a word as Jack alternately excoriates and coddles him in front of a smoky set so painterly and still that it looks like a cheap backdrop. When Jack suddenly turns to run to catch his train, however, this cardboard set is shown to be real, swallowing up the figure which diminishes in the rear plane while Georgie looks on, forlorn.

Jack's exit is multiplied endlessly across all the films of Orson Welles, the close-up figure leaving to the rear, pushed to nothingness by a wide-angle lens. Welles' space is a vast tunnel. Seldom do characters enter or leave from the wings; more often the lens and lighting accentuate their feebleness as they pass out of view, even, indeed especially, after they have delivered an impressive speech in close shot. A dark wind ushers everything out the back of the frame so that the great baroque world of Kane, the splendor of the Ambersons, the palpable pleasure of the Boar's Head, are all blown away from us out the window of the screen, dispersed into the infinite nothingness of an expanding universe. Shot after shot insists on this as close-up figures gradually or suddenly lose their control of the scene in favor of the space behind them, space that refuses to amplify their sentiments, swallowing them up instead.

Citizen Kane is full of such scenes, almost defying the spectator to guess the full size of the set. Bernstein reads a legal document in close-up [4-6]; when he puts the pages down, Thatcher is shown to be sitting across a table from him in midshot; only then do we hear Kane's voice as he moves from a tiny figure by the window at the back of the room toward the desk to properly compose a three-shot. Earlier Kane as a young boy is photographed with his sled in standard medium shot, exterior [1-3]. Gradually the camera begins to pull back to reveal first his mother at the window, then Thatcher, then his father, the adults retreating with the camera to an interior room where they discuss the fate of the tiny boy still visible through the small rectangle of the window. At the end of the film, of course, we have the much reproduced static shots of Susan Alexander in Xanadu, building her puzzle on a set designed inhumanly by Citizen Kane himself [11, 12].

Such a spatial structure permits first of all a pervasive irony to color both *Citizen Kane* and *The Magnificent Ambersons*, as central characters are "put in their place" after dominating the frame [7-10]. The opening sections of *Ambersons* trades on this tone, so much so that we are led to believe the film will be a comedy of manners or a satire. The off-screen narrator situates quaint images for us, and (once little Georgie graces the screen) the images themselves are composed for comic effect, as when the boy runs down a man planting his garden.

Such easy ridicule continues into the ball sequence where Georgie's pretensions are mocked by the long shots that contain them. But at the end of the ball a new, more serious tone is signaled by Bernard Hermann's dark score rising up behind the hushed urgency of all the characters saying their good-byes. Isabel leads the camera to the exit where she is silhouetted against the door's leaded glass [14] while we see Georgie and Lucy engaged in making arrangements for tomorrow. At the same time, on the side of the screen Fanny and Jack whisper, watching Eugene take his leave of Isabel. The multiple desires and restrictions at play here are uniformly qualified by the somber lighting and by the dissolution that the decentered, mobile composition implies. No longer is the comedy of the film so pure as it had been. Georgie, Jack, Wilbur, and Fanny all say good night to each other poking good-natured jibes into one another's weak spots, but a deadening silence outlasts their chuckles. Moreover, deep shadows against the huge ceilings and voices yelling out distantly "Will you shut up in there" put us in a sepulchral space. Fanny and Georgie whisper loudly as one might at a funeral. Even the glorious sleigh ride which follows succumbs in the end to a dark iris closing down on the sleigh and all its passengers as it passes by a lone tree atop the distant hill [15, 16]. The iris is as quaint and as winning as the tradition of the sleigh ride itself. The technique and the tradition are both lost; indeed the technique signifies the loss. As if to seal this point Welles fades in next with the leaded door we saw at the end of the ball. This time shadowy figures approach from the outside. This time it is Wilbur's wake, not a Christmas ball, which is celebrated. In this, the film's first death, we are returned to the tomblike space of *Citizen Kane* and to a certain metaphysical serious-ness which ridicules the pretensions of the characters and even overwhelms the narrator himself and his irony. "George Am-berson Minafer had got his comeuppance"; so does every viewer who thought to laugh at this boy and at this era from the enlightened distance of modernity. Welles would hurl all of us, all boys and all eras, into a space of doubt and inevitable loss.

These hints of darkness are fulfilled toward the film's end in one of Welles' most frightening and masterful scenes. Fan-ny's latent madness finally overbrims itself as she confesses her destitution to Georgie and her fear that he will "leave her in the lurch." This once proud woman sinks to the floor in complete despair. Georgie, befuddled at her loss of strength, tells her to stand up, not to burn herself against the boiler she is leaning up against. "It's not hot. It's cold," Agnes Moore-head blurts out. No music moderates the abrasiveness of this ugly scene, as Georgie finally pulls the woman down a corridor through two sets of doors and into the great drawing room where now all the furniture stands covered in white sheets. Fanny's helpless sobbing brings an era and a film toward its close, even as Georgie tries fruitlessly to comfort her. The scene as a whole expresses in full pathos the disintegration and loss that has obsessed Welles in all his films. And the tenacious camera which stays with the entire scene imitates this process of decay as we are pulled without a cut from the floor by the dirty boiler through the house we have come to know so well and, in a final whirling gesture, into an inhumanly distant view of Georgie and his aunt lost in the deep shadows of the hollow drawing room.

The seriousness of this scene sits badly with the glossy sentimental ending repudiated by Welles.[4] And no wonder! This was the director whose very first project was the scuttled *Heart of Darkness*. His has always been a cinema of penetration, not of surfaces. His very first images as a filmmaker announce this ethos as the camera takes us ineluctably forward toward Kane's eerie castle while deep chords set a nearly metaphysical tone. This film, and all his subsequent work, we suspect, will be about mysterious penetration into a horrifying depth. Comedy, irony, parody, and satire will enter, but all will be buckled under the framing chords of the "power music,"[5] and the preternatural movement of the camera. Even in the silliest and safest episodes, we stand ready to be taken away by the music and the solemn crane of the camera.

The opening and closing of *Citizen Kane* are exemplary in figuring the plunge into a drama and the plunge of that drama. In a single movement they figure the strategy of *transition* by which a massive façade is penetrated to its hollowness, a strategy we have seen elaborated in the tactics of mise-en-scène, of narrative structure, and of character development. If Welles' narration (what we have termed his bravura) strikes us at first as pompously loud, it is only so he can hear its echoes pathetically die away.

"I WROTE and directed this film; my name is Orson Welles." His voice leaves the most lasting impression even as the image of the microphone swings away from us at the end of *The*

---

⁴ The interested reader may learn more about the making of this and all of Welles's films in Charles Higham's *The Films of Orson Welles* (Berkeley and Los Angeles: University of California Press, 1970). Naremore's book is full of other details as well and is highly recommended.

⁵ Naremore, *Magic World*, p. 77.

Magnificent Ambersons. Welles' voice is resonant and volu-
minous, satisfyingly thick. It is, as much as possible, the voice
of God, confident because omniscient, demanding that we
hearken to it and interpret our situation in relation to its
message. If this feeling is greatest in *The Magnificent Ambersons,* where paradoxically he hides behind the camera, it emanates just as surely from his other films: the booming voices
of Kane, Hank Quinlan, the Advocate, and Gregory Arkadin;
the subtly modulated roles which that voice adopts in the
Shakespeare films where he would render up to eight different
parts. Because of the genius of his own voice and the experience this gift opened up for him first in the theater and then
in radio, Welles was able to break decisively with Hollywood
sound practice and to give to his films a new tone bearing an
unaccustomed feeling.

Welles' sound practice is first perceived as a problem to be
overcome. Particularly in his European films, dialogue is so
muffled that in many instances it is incomprehensible at first
hearing. This has always been attributed to the cheap post-
synchronization his budgets required. Yet we find already in
the RKO films the first seeds of a conception of sound neces-
sitating increased audience acuity. Dialogue overlaps would
seem to be the key to this new method, but more central is
Welles' practice of microphone placement in conjunction with
the overlaps. *Citizen Kane* and *The Magnificent Ambersons*
abound in examples in which a close-up voice will unexpect-
edly smother a conversation taking place at mid-distance, or
where a boisterous exchange will be followed by whispering
or sobbing. Altogether these oppositions produce a veritable
audio space in which events take place. Obviously adopted
from the techniques spawned by dramatic radio production,
this spatializing of the sound track is built up through throat-
miking for whisper effects, apparent directional sound, reverberation, and high-level ambient noise inclusion. Such extended space is put into play in conjunction with a heightened
use of the conventional "sound off." In the Amberson mansion
voices emanate from unseen rooms (the good-night scene after

the ball) and huge doors echo when pushed closed off-camera. Sound so dominated Welles' conception of this film that most sequences are designed to integrate audio information with the fewest possible camera positions. We have mentioned already the single-take sequences in the kitchen, at the train station, and of the Major before the fire. These are static scenes, readily accessible to the single angle. Welles goes beyond this in certain action scenes where one couple walking in conversation will pass out of view urging the camera to pick up what the sound track is already giving to us, a second conversation of a second couple. It is the flow of conversation that dictates the rhythm of this film and the role of the camera. Doubtless, over the course of ninety minutes a much larger, more atmospheric space is represented than we are accustomed to, thanks to which this comedy of manners, this satire, can affect us with unusual power.

Touted for his expressionist visual sense, Welles' most signal moments come to us from devices realized on the sound track. When placed counter to the image, the voice delivers rhetoric or irony, as in the haughty recitation of the Holinshed Chronicles or in the narrator's judgment toward the end of *Ambersons*: "George Amberson Minafer had got his comeuppance, had got it three times full and running over." On other occasions the sound track, far from smugly commenting on what we see, is the very vehicle of pathos: Welles' most outrageously authoritative voice screaming, "You can't do this to me Gettys. I'm Charles Foster Kane," the murmurs following Isabel Amberson's death, the train whistle calling Jack away after her funeral, the phone call Tania makes prefiguring the downfall of Quinlan, Quinlan's own voice betrayed by a walkie-talkie in the final moments of *Touch of Evil*, Joseph K. pleading for justice to a raucous courtroom in *The Trial* and the pathetic ditty sung as he awaits the blast of the dynamite. Added to all these scripted effects is the continual friction of ambient noise and choral voicing which thicken the image, dragging it toward its slow decline.

Welles' fascination with the possibilities of sound culminates in his *Chimes at Midnight*. Perhaps the greatest adaptation of Shakespeare that the cinema has yet produced, this is also the adaptation most difficult physically to hear. Lines are delivered at lightning speed, often over the shoulder, mixed with the dialogue or laughter of other characters, by quick turns bellowed, then murmured. Some viewers find it maddening to find our greatest poet left to the mercy of Welles with his bizarre sense of sound mixing and of pace. They prefer the Olivier films where every speech is directed to the audience, amplified by the closed shell of its decor, separated from neighboring speeches by studied silences if not actual changes in camera setup. In this way we miss not a line; indeed we might think of *Henry V* or *Hamlet* as films based on Shakespeare's *writing* whereas *Chimes at Midnight* is tied to the actor's *voice*. *Henry V*, especially, with its Duc de Berry sets, is an embellishment of a sacred text, truly a manuscript illuminated by the three-strip Technicolor filmstock and by the bright light of the projection arc [frontispiece]. In contrast, Welles violated the sanctity of the manuscript, piecing and patching a single film from the fragments of five different plays. Instead of a *text* which comfortingly remains behind the scenes and outlasts the film, Welles gives us a *voice* disconcertingly disappearing over time. Welles has taken as his model not the immortal Bard but "a poor player that struts and frets his hour upon the stage and then is heard no more."

Shakespeare, even Shakespeare, cannot outlast deterioration in time and diminution in space. Once again Welles has put forth an immense power, here the greatest dramatist the world has known, only to listen to it echo away inconsequentially in an infinitude of natural space and time. The effect is the more disturbing for the simplicity of its means. Whereas the techniques of transition, of embedding, and of parable all depend upon the magician's panoply of tricks, Welles also knows how to devastate through sheer sound recording.

Far from betraying theater, cinema here bestows upon it a most intimate gift, to let its cultured speeches contend with the wind of a truly open space, to test human struggle in the vast stretches of inhuman time. Recall Gielgud as the king in his cold, enormous castle [21], Hotspur spewing forth heroic epithets on the windy hill, or Falstaff discoursing white-robed in the birch forest ... the words of all these die out as we hear them, are carried away by the wind they cannot hush [22]. Thus, the nostalgia expressed in the prologue ("Where have they all gone? Dead, all dead") comes through the sound track to haunt every moment of the film. Only the Holinshed Chronicles, read imperiously by Ralph Richardson, pretends to outlast the events it comments on. Yet this is precisely that official view of history and of life satirized by the human life of the Boar's Head, by the flesh of Shakespeare's verse, and by the raspiness of the actors delivering that verse. Despite its victory over impersonal monumentality, such realism pays a price, the price of transition, deterioration, and mortality. Welles' great reverberating laugh is locked within the body of Falstaff borne off in a box at the end to be lowered deep into the earth [24].

DESPITE his background in theater and the evident theatricality of his personality, Orson Welles is fully a man of the cinema, if by this we mean someone whose most profound realizations are made possible in this medium. The illusory quality of the image, the magic-trick effects of motion picture technology, the depth of sound, and the shallowness of the screen all contribute to the expression of Welles' meditations on authenticity, mirage, impermanence, and loss.

First Bazin and now Roland Barthes have written evocatively of the relation of photography to death.[6] The image is the trace left by an object gone before us in time. More than representing that object, it expresses its absence. And yet the animating power of motion confers on the cinema a vibrancy missing from the still photograph. Barthes recognized this in

---

[6] André Bazin, "The Ontology of the Photographic Image," *What is Cinema?* (Berkeley and Los Angeles: University of California Press, 1967), pp. 10-15. Roland Barthes, *Camera Lucida* (New York: Hill and Wang, 1980).

his classic formulation: "Film can no longer be seen as animated photographs: the *having-been-there* gives way before a *being-there* of the thing."[7] Popular criticism supports Barthes' distinction. Movies are thought of as the artform that captures life, brings to life, animates our dreams, and so on.

Welles is one of those few directors (Truffaut is another) whose overriding obsession with the past and death goes against the grain of the medium even while it is best expressed in that medium. How does he distort the moving image to make it figure its own demise? We have already encountered his most calculated strategy for this in the embedded story. By consigning his images to a teller, especially when that teller is representing a past event, Welles manages to frame what we see like an expanded still photograph. The images of Kane at the newspaper office or at the opera or at Xanadu may affect us greatly but part of what we feel about them is their distance from us. Unable to break out of the temporal boundary constructed for them, they are the property of the teller who recounts them. Once again Welles plays with the tension between power and debility, this time between the strength of living pictures and our realization that these are of the past.

Doubtless this tension gives to *Chimes at Midnight* a sentiment absent even from the Shakespearean original. Not only is the life at the Boar's Head contrasted with the tomblike empire at the court, that life has already been put into the realm of memory by the rueful preface where two old men reflect upon the days that they have seen, all gone. The film then operates under two time schemes, that of the eternal history of the Plantagenets as chronicled in the heroic language of Holinshed, and that of the mortal history of Falstaff and the common folk, livingly expressed in the human verse of Shakespeare. We must add to this that other nostalgia for Shakespeare himself which Welles is able to inject into the

[7] Roland Barthes, *Image, Music, Text*, trans. Stephen Heath (New York: Hill and Wang, 1977), p. 44.

film, a regret for a time now gone when life and history could be so completely and satisfyingly represented.

In all his films the images arrange themselves in such a way as to embody the notion of loss and death. They obliterate themselves in the characters' flow away from the camera, in the deep shadows that settle on them, in the contrived quaintness of their presentation, and of course in the architectural structures that dominate the compositions (sepulchral rooms, old castles, timeless and inhuman spaces).

We watch Welles' films not as living artifacts emerging into our present, but as traces of a power that once was. We want to be astounded by the strength of that power even while the greater power of time reduces this strength to dust, to memory. While it is true that Welles indecorously promotes this reading of his films through overt references to death and loss lodged in the dialogue or contributed by the morbid voice of the narrator, the tone of the past and of things passing is constantly maintained by the work of the sound track. For an image is always potentially graspable, sight being, as Walter Ong urges, a most possessive sense as it seizes views like postcards.[8] But sound is the sense of hearkening, of vocation. Its source remains outside us, profoundly in the Other. When, as in Welles, this source retreats from us, we are left with a nostalgia for the full-throated presence left in its echo on the sound track. In short, unlike the simple pastness of the still photograph, Welles' films are simultaneously grand and gone; we are present to their fading.

To characterize this effect critics have called upon a series of spatial metaphors: the cavernous volume of his images, the screen as window onto a vanishing point which swallows up the figures that had loomed so large. Our meditation on sound and on temporality suggests other, potentially corrective metaphors. These films do not dwell on something that once was close and now is far away; instead their source, like some

[8] Walter Ong, *The Presence of the Word* (New Haven: Yale University Press, 1967), pp. 166-68.

original vibrating chord, is settled deep within them, producing a tone which, through successive borrowings, modulations, usages, and distortions, is transformed into the gaudy surface of the films. But the inauthenticity of this showman's technique still serves as a great volume for the vibrations of life within it. In other words, the very hollowness of Welles' personal world view, the emptiness of his paradoxes, his characters, and his tricky plots, prepares us for the sound of something in its core.

Although unrecoverable in literal fact, it is wrong to suggest that this something (this authentic feeling or formulation) is utterly lost in the past. For the tense of Welles' films is never that of the simple past, but of the historical preterite. No event in his film floats free; all are bound up in an historical account which Heidegger would call "recollection in care."[9] And even when, at his most relentless, as in *Chimes at Midnight* or *The Magnificent Ambersons*, he questions the very histories that hold the past so dear, Welles effectively encloses time in the giant box of his narration. He may no longer feel able to touch the real life of Merrie England, nor that of Shakespeare, but he can allude to them, or rather (to maintain our metaphor) he can permit something of their sound to vibrate the empty space he has fashioned around them.

He has, in both senses of the term, *related* something to us. In this way his films are repetitions of a care about mortality, repetitions to which we can now add our own meditation which is related to and relates his subject. The cultural extension this produces is, Ricoeur would suggest, an artistic compensation for the essentially nontransferable character of death.[10] If our criticism is a mere echo of his films, Welles' corpus itself issues up an echo of art and through art the tremolo of something feeble but authentic by which we sense both feeling and life.

[9] Martin Heidegger, *Being and Time*, trans. Macquerrie and Robinson (New York: Harper & Row, 1962), pp. 437, 438.
[10] Paul Ricoeur, "Narrative Time," *Critical Inquiry* 7 (Autumn 1980), 188-90.

CHAPTER TEN

The Passion of Identification in the Late Films of Kenji Mizoguchi

REPRESENTATIVE both of artistic grace and social rebellion, women are at the center of virtually every film Kenji Mizoguchi made, pursuing the values of futile revolt and tragic acceptance which he himself prized. He filmed them implacably with unblinking eye until they would stare back accusingly as at the end of *Sisters of the Gion* and *Osaka Elegy*. But he also filmed them sympathetically in pathetic surroundings and with unquestionable feeling in the movement of his camera.

How can we put together the rebellious social side of Mizoguchi with the nearly stoic metaphysical side? When Okita, at the conclusion of *Utamaro and His Five Women*, murders her lover and his mistress and then prepares to end her own fated existence, she tells Utamaro that she has practiced in her life what he developed in his art, a refusal of all compromise and a drive to go to the end of an action no matter what its consequence. If women have revolted against the system of prohibitions, exchanges, and hierarchies established by men with the congenital blindness suited to the self-centered banality of their ambitions, it is because women alone see right through to the end of this system, sensing its futility. If they have anything to teach us, it is the transpersonal, transhistorical, essentially artistic comprehension of the absurdity of such existence. Their vision goes well beyond those responsible for their personal plights. They see through the system, through the audience, and into the structure of an impersonal cosmos. Revolt thus leads the way to a kind of stoic contemplation which in his late films Mizoguchi pursued with fanaticism.

While certain male characters embody one or the other of these functions (think of the "sacrilegious hero" of the Taira clan saga or of the essentially passive artist-hero of *Ugetsu*), only Mizoguchi's females unite these impulses and do so to a degree that is beyond expression. As artist and iconoclast, Mizoguchi takes his inspiration from the stories he tells and the actresses who portray these stories for him. His least heroine, we feel, has gone further than reform or art. In their very way of walking is asserted a comprehension not even a lifetime of art could equal. Mizoguchi was obsessed with the gait of women, with their swoons, with their averted or penetrating gaze.[1]

The dual nature of his women, and Mizoguchi's fluctuating attitude toward them (recording them naturalistically only later to identify with them), pose special requirements for the viewer. At the same time this offers a potential and rare reward by providing an interval in time and space within which the spectator can move, oscillate. This is the interval between the borders of *identification* and *interpretation*, an interval that encourages us to rethink some of the key aesthetic issues of our era.

It is precisely the absence of such an interval that contemporary philosophers and critics have tried to expose in western fiction and film. Identification has been analyzed as an effect of a text striving to produce the illusion of presence and plenitude with the emptiness of differential signs. Under the banner of deconstruction contemporary criticism has waged a war against the illusions of identification and of full representation, whereby the spectator is overwhelmed by an undeniable picture of reality. Against such standard art a tradition of modernism is promoted: Lautréamont over Zola, Mayakovsky over Gorki, Vertov over Vidor, Oshima over Kurosawa. Mod-

[1] This idea was developed in a remarkable essay by Alain Masson, "Revers de la quiétude," *Positif*, No. 212 (November 1978).

ernism has come to mean the arbitrary play of signs in a text
that promotes the free construction of meaning. The viewer
or reader's relation to such a text is one of strong reading
("rewriting" in Roland Barthes' vocabulary), the absolute
contrary of the slavish passivity of identification.

Among film scholars Noël Burch has long been in the vanguard of the deconstructionist project. Not only has he tried
to expose the mechanisms of illusion and representation, he
has actively proposed alternative models of filmic signification: specifically the silent era before 1920, the current avant-
garde, and, most important for us, the prewar cinema of Japan.[2] Mizoguchi is a key figure in Burch's view of Japanese
cinema. Before the war he, along with Ozu, developed and
sustained a totally non-Hollywood narrative film tradition.
After the war he can be cited as among those Japanese directors who not only succumbed to western modes of representation, but who pandered to western tastes, groveling for the
lucrative export market.

Burch's rhetorical project leads him to bisect the world of
texts into those complicit with a dominant (Hollywood) version of reality, featuring illusion and identification, and those
other texts that ascetically abjure the temptations of this method
and its obvious rewards. Its moralism aside, Burch's view of
Japanese cinema and of Mizoguchi in particular remains crudely
on the surface. Mizoguchi's postwar films may indeed have
reached an export market and may indeed employ the lure of
identification, not to mention a compellingly delicious pictorialism, but these devices don't exhaust the project of his
films. That project might best be termed a "cinema of responsiveness." A machine of recording, the camera can also
become an instrument of response to what is recorded. This
mélange of objectivity and affect situates Mizoguchi's aesthetic within the problematic of reading and interpretation.
Specifically, Mizoguchi treats his subjects as texts whose il-

[2] Noël Burch, *To the Distant Observer* (Berkeley and Los Angeles: University of California Press, 1979), esp. chaps. 1-3, and 20.

lusions promote in him the need to respond in such and such a way. Identification with the illusion, then, is only the first part of an arc that ends in productive interpretation. Hence his films, especially the late ones, never pretend to touch ground and always point to themselves as textual experiences. While this should attract Burch and the deconstructionists, Mizoguchi's responses, his readings, have nothing of the anarchic about them. His films are disciplines in reading, the results of which, as every viewer of *Ugetsu* will attest, are as compelling and inevitable as the most tightly plotted Hollywood film.

While we do not go through Mizoguchi to something seemingly solid beyond, he gives us the solidity of his response to a text that hovers as an illusion before him. In Mizoguchi (and, Barthes has argued, in Japan generally)[3] there is never a question of pure reality to transmit nor of some independent Nature which the heroic artist may journey to and bring back to share with his spectators; instead there can only be the purity of the reading of a text about reality, that is, the productive reaction to an illusion. Every reading produces a reaction which in turn can be read as a text. Thus eddies out the infinite text of culture. The curiously mixed feelings of Mizoguchi's films are a measure of this intermediate stance between illusion and interpretation, the product of the "full emptiness" we are made present to, especially in *Ugetsu, Sansho the Bailiff, The Life of Oharu,* and *Miss Oyu.*

THE concluding camera "fixation" in each of these films transcends the drama that leads up to it. This is not the authorial transcendence of the tidy rhetorical flourish, nor an ironic comment on the action, but the completion of another action which has been operative throughout the film, that of the filmmaker's sympathetic reading of the destiny of his characters. Identification, in the generic sense of the term, acts as a relay between separate levels of the text, essentially between

---

[3] Roland Barthes, *The Empire of Signs*, trans. Richard Howard (New York: Hill and Wang, 1982).

separate texts. At the first level the character is created via actor identification with the role or circumstance of the script. To assure this, Mizoguchi's actresses were forced, for months before their role, to wear the costume of the period, to frequent museums, and to listen to the music of the time.[4]

His well-known refusal to cut within an action can in part be attributed to the respect he accorded the player's identification with her role. One might be tempted to suppose that the camera struggles to follow and amplify the actress's reading of the role if it were not for the fact that Mizoguchi's most elaborate movements are those that, though beginning with an actor's movement, continue until they reach a new, distinct, and settled composition all their own. And so although characters control the framing of shots, always finish the actions they begin, and usually initiate whatever movements the camera does make, the audience soon identifies with the camera via its quasi independence. This independence is also attributable to the aestheticized compositions of many scenes and to the noticeable ellipses between actions. To put this all together, the viewer must read the camera's response to an actress's response to her situation. Nor does it stop here, for the presumably originary situation she identifies with is often itself a textual response (in the form of legend, story, poem) to a hypothetical reality so far back it is literally out of the picture.

The Life of Oharu suitably exemplifies these strata and the movement of identification that interrelates them. The camera watches Kinuyo Tanaka come to terms with the role of Oharu, derived from one of Japan's greatest literary classics, Saikako's *Life of an Amorous Woman*. This seventeenth-century tale, essentially satiric and picaresque, chronicles the foibles of an easy woman who stumbles morally over and over to the delight of the reader. Tanaka, reading this tale from the perspective of postwar Japan, projects a tragic pathos in the grace

---

[4] Readers interested in a critical and biographical overview of Mizoguchi, or in discovering sources to find out more about his films, should consult Dudley and Paul Andrew, *Kenji Mizoguchi: A Guide to References and Resources* (Boston: G. K. Hall, 1981).

of her falls, a grace so transcendent that she is permitted to escape society altogether in a final fall to the role of an indifferent mendicant nun.

This notion of role operates beyond the obvious technical requirements of the cinema, for the character, Oharu herself, conceives of her life as a series of roles in which she has participated. The flashback structure of the film guarantees this attitude of "reinhabiting" situations, allowing feelings to well up out of memory. In the opening segment she enters a temple to stare at a constellation of statues of famous Bodhisattvas. Focussing on one of these, she sees in its stony face the visage of Toshiro Mifune, her former lover executed for love of her. A glance-object structure (including the film's single close-up shots) underlines the primacy of this moment as trigger for the film to follow. She identifies, if not with Mifune, then with the past in which he played the decisive role. More important, her hallucination not only produces the image that permits the film of her life to unroll, it produces as well a reaction from her. In one of cinema's most gracefully telling gestures, her head cocks sadly and she slowly pulls the scarf from her hair [1]. The liquid slipping of this silk down the side of the screen is her response to the reading of the image before her. It is the prototype for numerous falls she will have throughout the film and for the equally numerous camera descents by which Mizoguchi will sympathize with her plight (after the family's exile at the bridge [7, 8], after the beheading of Mifune [3-6], after the suicidal run of Oharu). We can go so far as to say that just as Oharu's reactions to her situation are more important than the events that produced them, so Mizoguchi's reaction to Oharu transcends her tale. That tale begins with the distant camera set before a carefully raked palace garden while Oharu and her small entourage pass before us in extreme long shot [2]. It ends with Oharu continuing to pass screen left out of frame, this time alone, as the camera remains still on the elegiac temple in the distance [9, 10]. She has entered and passed completely through Mizoguchi's view, our view. We have used her as the pretext

for our own movement, just as Tanaka, as actress, used Sai-
kaku's novel as pretext for her performance. Thus goes the
dialectic of indentification and interpretation.

Oharu may be Mizoguchi's most rigorous and complex
film, but in terms of the question of identification it is far
simpler than some of the later masterworks. It clearly exhibits
the paradox of distance and involvement which defines the
experience of his films. The *distance* comes not merely from
camera placement but from Mizoguchi's determination to let
every action run its course and to separate each action with
tangible intervals. The *involvement* derives from Mizoguchi's
peculiar timing which insists on a certain view of an action
and waits for it to erupt, as though the camera itself were a
bellows stirring the embers of the dramatic interplay to ignite
in sudden flame. Each scene has its own dramatic structure
and runs to its own fiery conclusion. The camera flourish
which concludes so many of these scenes is an expression of
the involvement that demands and results from this kind of
obsessive uninterrupted look.

Sansho Dayu forthrightly takes up the questions of identification and sympathy in relation to the status of texts. Instead of a single character with whom we and the camera
must come into relation, *Sansho* presents us with a family
who exchange sympathy via identification through texts. In
the first sequence mother and son exchange a memory about
the father's trauma of exile. The mother recalls their last moments together when the son received an heirloom from his
father along with the sacred text, "Be merciful to all men."
A dissolve returns us not to the mother but to the son wearing
the heirloom and speaking of his father. His spirit and love
is thus shared. In the film's closing scene this same mother
and son will again merge in repeating the father's text. The
route which the film follows to permit this conclusion involves
a set of exchanges too intricate to detail here. What is crucial
to note, however, is that these exchanges occur as the passing
on of texts. The mother's plaintive song from the island of
Sado is brought to the daughter via a slave girl. The memory

of the mother's cry "Anju, Zushio" wells up when the siblings repeat the cutting of the branch. Mizoguchi's camera here insists on the textualizing of this scene, making it not an action but the record of a meaning. This scene becomes a theatrical scene, read by its actors who change their lives in relation to the meaning it holds.

Sansho Dayu is a film about the emergence of morality out of a state of natural brutality. It is also about the centrality of texts and textuality in an illiterate and, consequently, unreadable world. When Zushio recognizes meaning in the text of a song, a dramatic reenactment, or the saying of his father, he frees himself from the meaningless activity of the slave camp, activity which by its very nature is unmemorable. Because they intone a text (the father's dictum), this forlorn couple, huddling alone on the beach out of sight even of the oblivious seaweed gatherer, rekindles the lost flame of culture and an idea of humanity.

Mizoguchi's position in this film is more direct and explicit than it was in *Oharu*. He actively joins scenes and memories. He himself memorializes and textualizes the activity of the family. Consciously the film participates in the proliferation of the father's text. The credits are themselves supered over two ancient sacred markers, present-day traces of the birth of meaning. When the slave girl from Sado sings the mother's song, she spins wool from wheel to wheel. Likewise the film unwinds in creating the fabric of the same plaintive hymn, passed on not directly but through the countless retellings the tale of Sansho has undergone, culminating in Mori Ogai's sensationally popular novel, the credited source of the movie.

If Mizoguchi's film seems disturbingly empty in the end, it is because he has audaciously placed his legend within the indifference of undramatic time. The seaweed gatherer exists in the state of nature, while the legend, dramatic and consequential, institutes cultural time, progress, and hope in the future. In identifying with Mizoguchi's weaving cinema we identify not with the success of culture and legend, but with the effort of textuality in an otherwise unreadable world. This is not a question of comedy versus tragedy since both of these are cultural constructions. In *Sansho* we participate in the eloquence of a meaningful gesture thrown up in the face of the indifference to which it arises in response. Once again identification is the key to the film and to our experience, but it is a knowing identification which places a burden of sympathy on the subject, refusing the consolation of fullness or presence. We are asked to identify with the difference of a text in the indifferent emptiness of the cosmos.

Can we continue to call this operation, by which an artist creates an image of a prior text, "identification," especially when the distance between the image and its subject is sadly insisted upon as it is at the end of all the films we have discussed so far? This kind of sympathetic participation by an observer in a primary scene is part of Japanese aesthetics generally and, therefore, lifts it out of the category of illusionism and passive identification.

Recall the horizontal panel paintings of the feudal era. Seldom is a scene of natural beauty rendered without the presence of an observer visibly meditating on or reacting to the view before him. The summer mountain scene may suggest or express "majesty" or "tranquility" or any of the highly coded moods permitted in Japanese art, but it will do so through an observer moved by this experience. Nature itself either cannot be trusted to deliver feeling or, more probably, is thought to express feeling only in the presence of a spectator.

Haiku poetry concentrates this same convention through the sequence of its rigid lines. A scene or action is presented in the first two lines, whereas the third line suddenly introduces a particular perspective, a human view or feeling. Listen to Bashō:

> The sound of a water jar
> Cracking on this icy night
> As I lie awake.

Coming closer to Mizoguchi's own interests and to the cinema, one would do well to start with the various aesthetics embodied in the *nō, kabuki, bunraku,* and *shinpa* theater. Many instances of each of these dramatic forms crop up in his films and we know that he was an addicted spectator all his life. A catalogue would contain many straightforward adaptations and even more instances of the partial inclusion of a theater performance in his films.

More important than direct reference to these forms of theater, however, is the model they provide for a kind of mediated artistic experience. Mizoguchi was to shape this model into his own complex narrative stance. At the very least he took from traditional theater the absolute separation of action and telling. Here most importantly, narration is sung from the side of the stage, accompanied by instrumental music which provides the scene with added aural mimesis (the sound of rain or of a battle), but which can also respond to the action or reflect upon it. In *bunraku,* of course, the visible presence of the puppeteers further mediates the performance and the tale it represents. In addition to these aspects of narration, the stories, sets, and acting in *kabuki* theater readily serve to accentuate heightened moments through a kind of concentration and counterpoint which Eisenstein was the first to recognize as a potential the cinema might adopt but which few filmmakers have dared to emulate.[5] In his own way Mizoguchi did dare, so much so that one might speak of his work as *performances* in film, including the performance of his actors which he was loath to interrupt through cutting, the performance of his camera which, in quasi-independent fashion, responds to the actors, and the performance of the music which both participates in the drama and reacts pathetically to its consequences.

The route of this aesthetic leads directly to Japan's unique contribution to early cinema practice, the *benshi.* Audiences came to watch not just a film, but a professional response to that film. The *benshi's* commentary related the tale, to be sure,

[5] Sergei Eisenstein, *Film Form* (New York: Harcourt Brace, 1949), pp. 19-27.

but from a distinct style and personal repertoire. This Japanese
penchant for separate but simultaneously presented texts, linked
by mood and thought, finds its champion in Mizoguchi. He
treated each of his collaborators as the maker of a finished
text which it was up to him, Mizoguchi, to play out in his
own medium and in his own way. This accounts for the stony
silence that notoriously signaled his dissatisfaction with a writ-
er's draft, a decorator's sketch, or an actress's run-through of
a scene. Refusing to impose his will in an area that didn't
belong to him, he nevertheless forced all to repeat and rework
their particular "texts" until they had surpassed themselves
and given him something at the peak of intensity and ex-
pressiveness, something with which he could identify and begin to interpret. Hence the paradox: Mizoguchi, at once the
most feared and exacting of directors, was also the one who
gave to his co-workers the fullest responsibility for creating
an acceptable artifact in their own fields of expertise.

   This view of the artist as disciplined craftsman infuses Mizoguchi's most personal and sustained meditation on the vocation of the artist, his portrait of Utamaro, the greatest of
the *ukiyo-e* printmakers of the eighteenth century. Mizoguchi
clearly admires the way the mass-produced aspects of the
ukiyo-e do not in the least detract from its instrumentality as
a means of refined expression. Utamaro is at once a popular
hero and an artist whose genius is capable of challenging the
greatest practitioners of graphics living in Japan. He works
in a frenzy for art equalled only by the passion for life which
his subjects, beautiful courtesans, play out to the fullest. He
exists within the heat of history and event, only he does so
with a calculated distance. His works immortalize the history
they seek to express, the passions that are so strong and sublime that it is at once inevitable and inconceivable that they
should pass away. The final credits roll over a torrent of prints
that rain down from above, each landing on and replacing
the one beneath, each memorializing a passionate scene from
the lives of the women who lived not with but around him.
What obsesses Utamaro and, through him, Mizoguchi, is not

the fleeting lives of the women, nor even the prints he makes of them, prints that are disposable and mass-produced; rather it is the activity of expression which through repetition and discipline is the way to vision and serenity.

The primacy of discipline and activity, that is, of artwork over artifact, lends prestige to popular arts and crafts, to pottery, printmaking, and the cinema. Mizoguchi surrendered himself to this ethic and this aesthetic, and sought to bring out in his films the fleeting vestige of such discipline. The Japanese critic Tadao Sato has demonstrated how intimately related to traditional Japanese arts is this Zen attitude of Mizoguchi, an attitude that crystallizes in the peculiarly Japanese effect of "impermanent posturing."[6] Unlike the classics of western cinema, Mizoguchi's films deliver neither clear statement, nor well-constructed drama, nor stable outline. Instead, he presents us with the *process* of coming to a peak of meaning, only to slip off in search of something further. This eloquently describes the feelings conveyed by his famous crane shots which, at the appropriate moment in the drama, glide into a perfectly expressive composition and then fall away after holding this posture for as long as is seemly.

The Zen philosophy that this camera strategy is said to express and the peculiar texture of his films that it helps describe are of less interest to us than its function as an important and challenging sort of identification. For this gesture of his camera carves out an intangible space which has no meaning of its own but rather is linked to a pretext that develops and itself disappears. This act of response, this co-expression, completes itself in the spectator from whom is demanded neither understanding nor judgment, but the permanent readiness of a distinct yet parallel response. Mizoguchi's films are not objects to be observed but textual acts putting in motion correlative acts of response.

[6] Tadao Sato, "On Kenji Mizoguchi," *Film Criticism* 4 (Spring 1980), 2-16.

I N what way is this style and aesthetic complicit with western representational models? What we have described as "impermanent posturings" and "fixations" of response, Burch accuses of mere pictorialism, catering to the West's facile understanding of Japan as a land of mystery and vague beauty where philosophers and artists wistfully ponder the evanescence of life. Certainly the overwhelming popularity in Europe and America of films such as Kinugasa's *Gate of Hell* with its pastel view of a traditional past gives substance to Burch's charge that Japan in the 1950s cashed in on an international hunger for delicious illusions. Over against the more dialectical, analytical films of the thirties whose subject matter was often socially relevant, these export "festival" films seem escapist and precious, exciting western audiences for that very reason.

But in his blanket condemnation of the rejuvenated Japanese industry, Burch blinds himself to the peculiar use Mizoguchi makes of the pictorialism his films undeniably include and the seductive illusions they just as undeniably tempt the viewer to succumb to. What Burch finds to be "academically decorative" and "opportunistic" is in fact a working past "decoration" in search of its authority and its value. What he claims is only a "contrived laying of certain traits of [Mizoguchi's] earlier system over the framework of Hollywood codes" might better be thought of as a meditation via those traits on the kind of suffering he explored in his social films of the thirties.

To see this at work one should begin with the first of these late films, *Miss Oyu*. Burch can hardly complain about Mizoguchi cashing in on a ready-made audience, for this film, a critical and box-office flop, sought to revive quite an unpopular genre, the Meiji period film. The project of this revival led him to give Mizutani's set design a most prominent function in the overall effect of nostalgia indicated by the story. More important still, *Miss Oyu* marks the first collaboration between Mizoguchi and Kazuo Miyagawa and initiates the studied use of the elegiac camera movements that enthralled the West in *The Life of Oharu* and that might be said to characterize the late films in general. *Miss Oyu* is the first in a line of films to take aestheticism to the limit in order to peer beyond it.

The source of the film goes a long way in distinguishing Mizoguchi's project from the norm, for *Miss Oyu* derives from one of Junichiro Tanizaki's most famous stories of his "art for art's sake period," *Ashikari*. Tanizaki in the 1930s represented precisely the sort of Japanese artist scorned by Burch. Westerners have always felt at home in his delicious sensual refinement, and in his evocative nature descriptions which invariably are seasoned with the metaphysical. His is a literature of small but stunningly subtle effects.

Ashikari is a perfect example of Tanizaki's philosophy of art for it begins and ends in search of nearly indescribable effects. The story of *Miss Oyu*, which is the narrative heart of this novella, actually comprises but one-half its pages. The remaining half is an elaborate introduction in which a tourist encounters a traveler on the evening of the traditional moon-viewing ceremony by the River Yoda. Tanizaki has carefully given over his narrative voice to an aimless pleasure-seeker, out to relish the landscape and enjoy the country cooking. The story of Oyu has no direct connection to him (or to us) except as a prop to heighten the sensual and psychological effects which he has sought that evening.

Indeed, the introduction is even further contrived by the fact that the interior narrator who tells our tourist the story is himself also an observer at a distance. Although we surmise (and are eventually told) that he is the issue of the romantic tragedy he recounts, his knowledge of that tragedy comes not from direct experience but from his father who told him of Miss Oyu years ago when father and son made their annual pilgrimage to gaze not just at the moon but at a noble lady playing the koto on the porch of her lakeside estate.

And so we approach the tableau of the revered figure, Miss Oyu, through Tanizaki, through the tourist, through the traveler he meets, and that traveler's memory of his father's tale.

Oyu is indeed a hazy moon of a lady casting her glow coolly
and from afar.

The tale surrounding Oyu only heightens her inaccessibility.
A woman of rare independence, she has smitten the heart of
Shinosuke, but being a recently widowed mother she is in fact
unavailable. Through a uniquely Japanese web of allegiances,
duties, and self-sacrificings, Shinosuke marries Oyu's young
sister Oshizu and the three establish an unconventional menage. This arrangement outlasts the scandal it causes, but when
Oyu learns that because of her, the married couple are living
like brother and sister, she is filled with remorse and marries
lovelessly. The couple disappears into a Tokyo slum where
Oshizu dies in childbirth; Oyu retreats to the lovely villa by
Lake Ogura passing her days in an atmosphere of melancholy
elegance. Everyone is drawn into this atmosphere: Shinosuke,
his son, and now even the tourist whose general sense of
sadness is defined and deepened by the story he has heard.
To this Tanizaki adds a characteristically haunting coda. Our
tourist looks from the moonlit landscape back to his inter-
locutor. "But where he had been sitting, there was nothing to
be seen save the tall grasses swaying and rustling in the wind.
The reeds which grew down to the water's edge were fading
from sight, and the man had vanished like a wraith in the
light of the moon."

The novella stops here, for our guide has succeeded in his
search; he has been surprised by the moonscape he went out
to see, a moonscape whose "haunting" beauty doubtless contains within it myriad ghostly tales. By this blurring of narrative and spectacle the "framed" tale of Oyu is not the novella's ultimate treasure, for it, too, has been used as a frame,
a narrative frame within which the landscape can evoke its
peculiar effects.

Tanizaki's effects are precious because they are invariably
directed to the single observer. The tourist's highly tuned sensibility is meant to lead our own into an atmosphere that
floods us with that eerie feeling of ghostly loss. It is precisely
this concentration, cultlike, on private sensation and mysti-

fication, which contributes to the suspicions of critics like Noël Burch who indict this aesthetic for its frivolity and uselessness. Neither art nor society is improved, disrupted, or even affected by such stories which nevertheless masquerade as serious.

In adapting *Ashikari* and particularly in enhancing the misty pictorialism of its already evocative imagery, Mizoguchi seems liable to Burch's charges. Yet his is by no means an "art for art's sake" aesthetic; rather it is art for the sake of peering past art's limit to that which precisely but namelessly bounds it. First of all, if Tanizaki aimed to manipulate private sensations, we must say that Mizoguchi's goal is to convey the *impersonal* character of emotion. To begin, he approaches the tale directly, eliminating all three interior narrators and (uncharacteristically) maintaining complete chronological sequence from the moment Shinosuke lays eyes on Oyu to his disappearance into the reeds beyond her lakeside manor. Furthermore, he distributes viewer identification among the three main characters by offering support through camera movement and point of view to Shinosuke, Oyu, and Oshizu in succession. This keeps us at bay, juggling our sense of the complex feelings involved and reserving our fullest identification for the camera view which outlasts its convergence with the views of any one character.

After the unraveling of the menage toward the end of the film, when Oyu retires to her manor and the couple moves to their Tokyo slum, the camera view asserts its full independence, almost lifting itself beyond the pathetic drama to a general view of human passion and suffering. The style associated with this project borders on the ritualistic. The sequence showing the couple's decline in Tokyo, for instance, opens and closes with symmetrical descriptive shots of the slum, where in the distance a steaming locomotive passes first left (nudging the camera to move aside) and then screen right [11]. Within these temporal and spatial brackets Oshizu dies in childbirth wrapped in Oyu's ceremonial kimono. This instance of dramatic economy is more than a case of understatement to quiet the audience before an explosive finale. It establishes the cool

and measured tone with which Mizoguchi brings this potentially torrid melodrama to its end, generalizing rather than
cashing in on its sentimental effects.

The final sequence opens with an elaborate tracking shot
approaching a picturesque lakeside villa. Circling up to a moon-
viewing party, we gradually distinguish Oyu and her retinue
of maidservants and artists as they perform sad music, consonant with the night [12]. A baby's cry sends her servants out
into the garden where they find Oshizu's infant and a letter
from Shinosuke. While Oyu reads this letter commending the
baby to her for life, the camera tracks from her face and down
across the full length of the koto lying next to her. Never has
a film insisted so literally on its own lyrical project. Although
nestled in nature, Oyu's villa is utterly artificial, as the delicate
shape of the koto, cut off from all background, testifies. Oyu
responds to this moment, the culmination of her life's sole
passion, in the only way she knows how, by asking her music
teacher to play a composition to welcome the new child brought
to her by the moon.

In a most daring coda, Mizoguchi frames a fully traditional
moonscape, his own "composition" responding to the drama:
on the misty moonlit lake, a boatman in the distance rhyth-
mically rows to deposit on the shore a silhouetted passenger.
A final tableau, the most painterly of Mizoguchi's entire career, places the hazy moon above a marsh full of rushes.
Shinosuke (for it is he) moves nō-like into the reeds singing
the traditional air he had shared in happier times with Oyu:

> Without you here
> Every time I think on it
> All seems melancholy
> Osaka and my life
> All the more unbearable.
> Don't think badly of me
> Our love was wrong.

Shinosuke recedes completely into the reeds leaving us in a
landscape which signifies bleakly the passing of man and of

love, and yet which signifies this so pathetically that it simultaneously insists on the presence of human feeling in the
earth itself [13-16].

Nature has become a sign that Mizoguchi both employs
and reads, a crucial paradox that takes us back to a remark
Oyu made in an early moment of triumph. After her exquisite
koto recital during which she had gone to great lengths to
create the proper atmosphere (with candles and incense), she
confesses that she barely enjoys her instrument. Instead it is
the pomp of the performance that she adores, particularly the
ornate Heien era kimono which she wears at once preten-
tiously and seriously.

Mizoguchi likewise overdoes the atmosphere, cloaking this
tale in an ancient, formal pictorial style and nudging its dramatic progression along in a hieratic rhythm. Music, light,
composition, and such traditional *topoi* as a boat, the hazy
moon, and the rushes of a marsh, concentrate the pathos of
the tale in the coda. But just as Oyu felt an authentic rapport
with an environment of her own construction, so Mizoguchi
can seriously respond to the desolate scene not just of spent
human passions but of their dissolution into a pictorial drama
of nature: moonlight on a somber marsh.

Here we can measure Mizoguchi's distance from Tanizaki,
for the filmmaker has obviously sought to reproduce the elements of the novel's final sentence "The reeds which grew
down to the water's edge were fading from sight, and the man
had vanished like a wraith in the light of the moon." The
sudden break which this passage signals in the novel between
a tale and the status of the teller (is he a ghost?) strikes us
with an icy eeriness. This is that singular effect which Tanizaki, following Poe, sought to produce in his narrator and in
his reader. But Mizoguchi's presentation of the same tableau
in no way seeks such a narrative twist. Instead this is the
fullest and baldest exposition of the aesthetic strategy that has
controlled the entire film, a strategy based once again on identification at a distance. The emotions that these final compositions indisputably arouse are so transpersonal in character

(opposed to the sensualism of Tanizaki) that we must question the power and use of identification.

The traditional garb of the moonscape, just like the Heien kimono, bears a definite feeling that we can neither resist nor call our own. Oshizu is happy to end her life enfolded in Oyu's gown, just as Oyu could feel most authentically herself in that gown's ancient aura, an aura, by the way, that Shinosuke and his sister claim belonged to their mother as well. In the same way, Mizoguchi is not being facile, as Burch no doubt would have it, when he calls up these ancient images out of his story; nor is he inventing a personal expression or one suitable to his characters. Instead, he is invoking an ancient ghost of nature, artificially bringing it up via the magnificent labor of actors, designers, and cameraman. Thus nature is a traditional and an exquisite mask through which paradoxically another nature appears, the bleak nothingness that outlasts the drama that produced it as an image. Transpersonal, even apersonal, emotion in Mizoguchi's aesthetics is a fact of nature, not of individuals, and his film produces out of the artifice of passion (a love story) a truly passionate artifice, this picture.

MIZOGUCHI's impersonal and indifferent mode of identification must make us question the concept itself. If we insist on defining identification as an illusion, we must do so now in relation to the "real illusion" of the cosmos as Mizoguchi saw it. If we only know reality through texts and only act in relation to our reading of them, then we must become adequate to the texts that precede us. Textuality is not arbitrary. The illusions of life have specific and developing contours and Mizoguchi succeeded in identifying some of those contours through the passion/action of his films.

Surely the proof of Mizoguchi's success in this method is the conclusion of *Ugetsu*. There his camera explicitly participates in the duping of the hero Genjuro who hallucinates the appearance of his dead wife upon his return to his empty home. But Genjuro retires to bed and the camera remains with the vision it has conjured up, with Miyagi who kneels before the fire and sadly does her mending. For several minutes we watch and sympathize with the ghost of Miyagi, waiting for the dawn sadly to sublime her into its white haze. What is remarkable here is not merely the paradox of presence and absence which the film has created, but Mizoguchi's willingness to learn from that paradox, his ability to adjust his sensibility to the sensibility of a phantom of his own creation.

Is this identification? And do the phantoms of his films likewise demand from us an identification that makes us adjust our sensibilities to them? I think they do, yet this is a very particular kind of identification indeed. Richard Wollheim, in his essay on identification in Freud,[7] distinguishes between the empathic and the sympathetic imagination, noting that we may suffer the same things as the subject of imagination or we may suffer in response to what we imagine the character to feel. Wollheim's explicit incorporation of the term "internal audience" within his notion of the imagination has even broader implications for film theory. Identification in his scheme can only be the name of a certain form of psychic potency, one in which our internal audience coincides with the subject of the imagination, as when I imagine my father and respond as I feel certain he would respond. Mizoguchi's method is quite other than this, coming much closer to sympathetic imagination wherein the internal audience is free to respond in its own way to a subject it nevertheless imagines in the strongest possible manner.

I have argued that this mode of identification is represented by the activity of reading, wherein two consciousnesses come together without coincidence across the body of a text. The results of this encounter are not pathological, locking us into the view of another; they are potentially therapeutic, expanding our range, shifting perspectives, allowing what Ricoeur

---

[7] Richard Wollheim, "Identification in Freud," *Freud: Essays in Criticism* (New York: Anchor Books, 1974).

aptly calls a complete redescription of reality from the parallactic vision that our crossover has made possible.[8]

But while avoiding the trap of pathological identification, Mizoguchi, we have seen, does not enter the camp and campaign ruled over by Barthes, Burch, and all the apostles of modernism who preach an ultimately solipsistic (de)constructivism. Mizoguchi provides a third way of dealing with a character, a text, and by extension with life itself. Through a studied discipline that permits the crossing over to another (a text, a person, a point of view) and a return to oneself, he imagines sympathetically in order to respond personally to the encounter. The object of imagination provides the rule for the response in much the way that, in Ricoeur's view, the semantic and syntactic aspects of a metaphorical combination provide a rule for interpretation. This doesn't mean that they point to a final or correct meaning; instead they invite us to roam in a new field of meaning but one that has been purchased for us by a pre-text.

In this way Mizoguchi's cinema performs the function that I consider most crucial for art in our epoch. Through the physicality and otherness of a set of signifiers, we are urged to entertain a new range of thoughts that promise to affect us. Captive neither of the artwork (traditional illusionism) nor of our own constructions (modernism), we adjust our sensibilities and potentially our lives to the rightness of something standing before us and inviting our imagination, inviting our sympathy, in short, inviting the gesture of our reading.

[8] Paul Ricoeur, *The Rule of Metaphor* (Toronto: University of Toronto Press, 1977). See especially Study 7.

CHAPTER ELEVEN

Conclusion: The Work of Cinema and the Art of Interpretation

MY nine studies, these thousands of words, are made possible by what motor, are directed by what authority? Without hesitation, look to the films themselves. For each stands out, has been made to stand out as extraordinary, that is, as Art. Whether through self-proclamation, through the designs their authors had for them, through the particular enthusiasm of their first audience, or through the discourse of the critical community (in journals, classrooms, conferences), these films have been pulled from the mainstream and offered to my aroused attention.

Thus Art is the motor of this book, for these are studies conducted in the aura of art, authorized by the discipline of criticism that thrives on and hopes to contain art's energy. That energy derives from difference, from the separation certain works enjoy from a mainstream of the ordinary. If the formalists are right to define the aesthetic as that function by which certain forms present themselves not for use or knowledge, but for their sheer and obstinate perceptual qualities, then we must pause and fawn over those few works that stand out from the countless stream of aesthetic objects fabricated by the industries of culture.

To promote or even consider the extraordinary one must tacitly hold a conception of the familiar. The standard Hollywood film has served as such a backdrop, the so-called transparent film of zero-degree style. But do such films exist except as a heuristic fiction? In considering *Meet John Doe* I concluded that every film held up for scrutiny exhibits flaws and tensions; every film struggles to stand on its own apart from the system that confers intelligibility on it. Hollywood is only one name for the regularity of this process of differentiation endemic to the culture industry of every nation and art form. As I noted in the Introduction, each of these films is feature length; each found its way to an audience through channels of distribution and exhibition. And so it wasn't only *Broken Blossoms* and *Meet John Doe* that succumbed to the normal mechanisms of meaning and pleasure; all these films found a waiting audience, a particular audience characterized, no doubt, by a high level of education and a familiarity with the arts, but an audience no different in function from that sought out by the kung-fu film or the Disney animated feature.

If all films live by a presumed difference from the norm, we must account for the difference that really makes a difference in those we choose to retain in our lives and to hold up as artistic. And this our century has most often done through the criterion of "difficulty" or "strangeness." All films may live in tension with the system but most capitulate readily to its rules of readability and its conventions of decorum. Others maintain a productive dissonance with the system that keeps an audience off guard in a search for meaning and value. When an audience believes this search is productive and that it is pointing toward an unnamed and unnamable solution outside the norm, they accord the work the highest value. If the difficulty is specious, as we sense in *Meet John Doe* and, to some extent, *Henry V*, charges of pretentiousness arise. If the difficulty is programmatically obtuse, as some claim to be the case in many avant-garde works, the search will be called off as inauthentic. Few audiences want to be taken for a ride in that way.

Formalists would catalogue types of films by their traits, enumerating kinds and quantities of differences among them, naming some films "familiar," others, "artfilms," still others, "avant-garde." The subcategories of these are potentially endless. But traits are only interesting to, and only interest, audiences. Paricularly when the categories are based on concepts such as "the familiar, the strange, and the obtuse" a notion of audience is essential. For differences count only when they are "taken as" different by a spectator.

Shall we jump to a sociology of art classifying not the films but the audiences who consume them in various ways and for varying purposes? Unquestionably the aura of art in which I find, experience, and discuss the films in this book has produced a certain kind of spectator with certain ambitious expectations. In an important way this book pays tribute to a socially privileged echelon of viewers, reinforcing the values already promoted by the genre of the artfilm. This value has been called into doubt as a mark of the leisured class, and these films have been criticized as a "spiritual commodity" that flatters a ruling class into believing in the authenticity and depth of life (or at least of its life). My study from this point of view might be taken as an exercise in self-deception and vanity; worse, it could be said to contribute to a vain and arbitrary system that represses other values, other classes. One needs a theory of culture (or at least a vision of one) to come to terms with issues such as these, for no film and no discourse is self-justifying. To return to the first question, it is the motor of "choice" that has engendered this discourse and others like it. What governs choice and what regulates the consequences of choice is a larger question we must next engage. But in any case, it should be evident that any film held up for study by that very fact will permit a discourse illuminating its value. I have chosen these films which, by involving the notion of art, chose themselves or chose me and others like me who are responsive to the claims and ambitions of art. Another audience may well choose a film or films thrown away by me into the stream of the ordinary. By pulling them from this stream viewers and critics not only keep them alive in culture but point to the fact that the whole stream is extraordinary and that there never was, except for argument's sake, a classic Hollywood or zero-degree cinema. But everything depends on "argument's sake," for audiences and the genres of films they respond to vie with one another in a competition of representations. Culture is nothing other than the field of such competition and the reckoning of the gains and losses of the various sides, together with the films that mean something to them. It is to the life of culture that we must next turn.

WHILE a complete sociological study of audiences, just like a complete formalist study of texts, can potentially exhaust the domain of the artfilm, accounting for its scope and place, neither gives a satisfying account. Neither involves itself in the struggle of films and views that makes up culture. Only a hermeneutics risks this far messier attitude in the hopes of participating in the experience of meaning by elucidating its possibilities and consequences. Only a hermeneutics tries to understand culture from the inside.

What is culture but the volume of texts harbored as valuable in any given epoch? It is the archive in which stand, catalogued or lost, those items that a culture can read and comprehend in a certain way and with a certain force. Thus meaning does not belong intrinsically to any film but is conferred upon it by the traditions (and within the conditions) of meaningfulness.

In my own case a particular discipline, that of critical studies, has permitted, encouraged, perhaps even forced the choice of films I have made and the mode of interpreting them I have pursued. And this very term "discipline," especially after its elaboration in the thought of Michel Foucault, suggests the urgency and strictness of cultural necessity over personal or natural predilection. What sort of talk goes on in our schools ushering in these films, letting them speak to us in ways that are both familiar or strangely enticing? It is certainly a talk that separates those who engage in it from the unschooled layman who frequents theaters in the mall to watch whatever Hollywood prepared that week or, more likely, who takes in TV sitcoms after dinner in the living room.

This book participates in a modestly short tradition of talk whose first chore is to maintain an enlarged archive of texts capable of engaging us. Beyond what is commercially available, films literally do exist in archives, saved by our concern from garbage cans, fires, or oblivion. We maintain them there, keeping them from crumbling into dust, cataloguing them so that they are at our command. This is an academic project carried on by scholars, buffs, and museums. Yet every culture and every subculture maintains, however casually and unconsciously, its own archive, those texts that it can draw upon and be interested in from whatever angle.

It is this notion of archive that Michel Foucault has taught us to pay attention to. Over and above any set of outstanding texts that might formerly have beckoned to us as the privileged indicators of a culture, the archive itself (its rules of inclusion, exclusion, hierarchy, organization, and legibility) tells us, he argues, what its principle of rationality is, thereby defining it as a culture.

Here enters Foucault's master concept, *power*, the unexplained and inexplicable driving force that permits one sort of culture to become dominant. In my case, one must question the authority of our school system and, particularly, of the nascent discipline of film studies that throws its weight in the direction of certain texts (artfilms, special genres, arcane primitive works) in competition with the dominant archive of sheer and crass entertainment.

The concept of power is infinitely more useful than that of archive, for it involves struggle, history, and momentum. In fact it turns the static image of the archive (as library) into the active and tendentious image of the canon. A canon protects a culture only after it is itself protected by rules for its proper understanding. In the most crucial cases (the Bible for a medieval world, Freud and Marx for today's academic world) the key text(s) are in the hands of expert exegetes who know how to read them. In other, less formal cases, there always exists what has come to be known as a "reading formation" that schools a culture in the proper "taking" of the texts that form its canon.

It is our interest, its kind and energy, that deposits texts into and withdraws them from the archive. While we needn't be aware of every item in the archive (since the very image of an archive suggests caches of potentially rich materials) we must be prepared to give our attention to whatever we locate within its vaults and chambers. But beyond the archive it is our particular "reading formation" that determines the types of textual experience possible in our era. We are disposed to certain expectations, goals, and methods in our encounter with texts and it is these which form the hierarchies of texts we value or dismiss. For whatever we concentrate on through our choice and our discourse is the value of a film. Those texts that have crumbled into dust and those still in the darkness of the vault are valueless to us today. Only when we expose a film and its workings to our sight and talk, only when it is handed down, does it become more than a document and enter the meaning-life we lead in culture.

Reading formation is another name for tradition, as tradition invokes or approaches texts. To realize that our predilections may not be natural but are inflected by what our tradition deems to be "balanced," or "tonal," or "excessive," or even "readable" is a humbling experience. Is it by accident or sheer will that certain films stand in the foreground today while others are in retreat or completely blocked from view? Is it by any moral or rational design that discussion about films flows in time with developments in culture? Are we to trust the developing scenario of discourse as it appears in journals, at conferences, and in course offerings, or are we to assume that this is the blind adventure of power and fad and that any real effort at value and meaning will have to come in spite of, not because of, the trends we cannot avoid?

CULTURAL philosophers and cultural critics are quick to point to their preferred principles of explanation here. The power that rules the direction of tradition comes from the workings of history, or from the interplay of class conflict, or from the dynamics of psychological pressures and their censorship. Without arbitrating these largest-of-all questions one can still point to the ubiquity of discrimination as a constant. Part of being human, a necessary part of the human being we can say, involves the making of choices about representations. Our "formation" as readers is thus not quite so arbitrary as many apostles of modernism would have it. Not only is it in our nature to engage texts, the choices we make as to what to read and how to read it, coming though it does from a tradition, depends on certain constants, the most obvious of which are biology and history. Our lives as sexed, always dying animals, tied to geography that involves horizons, seasons, and so on, limits the free play of reading and traditions of reading. More crucial, the fact that everyone, and most certainly the cultural historian or critic, is always already within tradition, makes history the chief guiding principle of reading. For all reading and all choices, including the most dispassionately scholarly or critical, take place in context, in that field of competing views we redundantly term culture.

Although critics continually remind us that psychoanalytic and ideological pressures call for and demand certain films (and certain values in all films) to be brought forth, these very psychological and ideological structures are themselves materially based in biology and history. In short, there is no escape from tradition, no utopian means of construing it from the outside. All we have to work on are texts and our interpretations of them in history. While we may argue over the effect and power of that "work" (some claiming we are the plaything of culture, others that we transcend or inflect culture) culture is the origin and end of our experience.

Thus the academicians who fight over the values of films and readings merely play out their age-old roles as conservators of culture or as firebrands of the new. This struggle, this competition between reading formations, is exactly what we know as cultural history, for the new always and only makes its appearance in tradition as part of that which is handed down.

It is hardly consoling to emphasize, as I have done, that our passion for films (especially for certain films) and that our discussions about them may amount only to a social necessity proceeding rather blindly down the alleys of history. One's view of history and culture will finally intervene, turning this into an animating or paralyzing realization. Paralysis results either from a too systematic or too skeptical view. In the great patterns imagined by traditional Christians, Marxists, genre theorists, and cultural determinists, history can only be the play of preestablished forces. In this view events (the encounter and discourse of films, for instance) assume if not an inevitable, then at least a redundant role. They interest such systematizers only as dispensable examples of a process beyond them. Strangely, the great skeptics of grand systems (and today we would have to name Jacques Derrida their leader) bring us to the same paralysis before the events of history, for no skeptic can expect anything of the new other than a recasting of the killing doubt.

Interpretation comes alive in the space between these extremes. A willing participant in cultural history, interpretation is undecided about history's value. In fact, only the oscillation between system and skepticism energizes its activity, activity that is always concerned with particulars. The experience of particulars that matter (of films, even, or especially, of certain films) budges one off dead center into the zone of competitive views and the history of interpretation.

This middle view isn't deaf to the bitter asides of the skeptics, but it sees skepticism as only part of a modern reading formation that may go out to encounter in films a discourse other than the purely academic conversation of cultural philosophers. For the systematic or critical philosopher, films can only be the object of inquiry and can at best be exemplary. But for those who choose to participate in a wider cultural conversation, films can be said to speak as subjects speak, not as examples. If we feel expectant about the possibilities within a book or film, then we are already engaged in a dialogue that involves skepticism and system but is not utterly ruled by either. More importantly, once we acknowledge that, in a manner of speaking, the films have chosen us, have stood out to us and demanded our attention and response, then our interest transcends ourselves.

Let us not be naive. Education, class, and era will push certain films into the fore and suggest approaches to those works. If culture is a conversation, we are only privileged to hear some of it at any one time and we are obliged to contribute our speech without benefit of knowing the whole. But we can nonetheless think of ours as a contribution. And, if we are prepared to live at all, we can trust, amid our doubts, that our choices of what to value and how to speak our values are not indifferent. Censorship displays by negative example that representations and discourse are never neutral and that in the struggle of history some representations and some interpretations are superior. Superior in what context? In the context of cultural history that ultimately envelops even those grand thinkers who seek to escape it. Theirs, after all, is only a contribution to academic discourse. We must listen to and be formed by them; but there are other discourses in the air and, for those of us so inclined, we will readily turn our partly formed hearing to the films that call to us.

Now if our listening to films seems to proceed by inclination and intuition, if our conversations initiated in the theater spill out with no clear conception of their destination but with a drive toward adequacy and eloquence, then we shall not hesitate to call interpretation an "art" and to be satisfied with it as a way, the best way, of participating in history. It is after all just as insubstantial and as important as the art of living.

INDEX

Library of Congress Cataloging in Publication Data

Andrew, James Dudley, 1945-
Film in the aura of art.

Includes index.
1. Moving-picture plays—History and criticism—
Addresses, essays, lectures.   2. Moving-pictures—
Aesthetics—Addresses, essays, lectures.   I. Title.
PN1995.A494   1984   791.43'75   84-1788
ISBN 0-691-06585-3

Dudley Andrew holds a joint appointment as Professor of
Communication and Theater Arts and Comparative
Literature at the University of Iowa and is the author of
Major Film Theories (Oxford),
André Bazin (Oxford), *Kenji Mizoguchi* (G. K. Hall), and
Concepts in Film Theory
(Oxford).